Palgrave Studies in Governance, Leadership and Responsibility

The fall-out from many high profile crises in governance and leadership in recent decades, from banking to healthcare, continues to be felt around the world. Major reports have questioned the values and behaviour, not just of individual organizations but of professionals, industries and political leadership. These reports raise questions about business corporations and also public service institutions. In response this new series aims to explore the broad principles of governance and leadership and how these are embodied in different contexts, opening up the possibility of developing new theories and approaches that are fuelled by interdisciplinary approaches. The purpose of the series is to highlight critical reflection and empirical research which can enable dialogue across sectors, focusing on theory, value and the practice of governance, leadership and responsibility.

Written from a global context, the series is unique in bringing leadership and governance together. The King III report connects these two fields by identifying leadership as one of the three principles of effective governance however most courses in business schools have traditionally treated these as separate subjects. Increasingly, and in particular with the case of executive education, business schools are recognizing the need to develop and produce responsible leaders. The series will therefore encourage critical exploration between these two areas and as such explore sociological and philosophical perspectives.

More information about this series at
http://www.springer.com/series/15192

Nehme Azoury
Editor

Business and Society in the Middle East

Exploring Responsible Business Practice

palgrave
macmillan

Editor
Nehme Azoury
Holy Spirit University of Kaslik
Jounieh, Lebanon

Palgrave Studies in Governance, Leadership and Responsibility
ISBN 978-3-319-48856-1 ISBN 978-3-319-48857-8 (eBook)
DOI 10.1007/978-3-319-48857-8

Library of Congress Control Number: 2016962631

Cover illustration: Daan Kloeg / Alamy Stock Photo

Printed on acid-free paper

This Palgrave Macmillan imprint is published by Springer Nature
The registered company is Springer International Publishing AG
The registered company address is: Gewerbestrasse 11, 6330 Cham, Switzerland

Acknowledgements

To my dedicated team, partners and colleagues, who made it conceivable to believe in a brighter future for our region.

To my family, who provided me with moral support throughout the writing of this book.

Contents

1 The Key Role of Media and Businesses in Helping Regional Societies Navigate Modern-Day Storms 1
Ramsay Najjar

2 Business and Organization for Sustainable Societies 17
Karim Seghir

3 Culture and Business Operations: How the Gulf Arab Leadership Style Impacts a Contingent Human Resource Management 31
William Scott-Jackson and Jonathan Michie

4 Development of Education and Its Impact on Middle Eastern Societies 49
George M. Jabbour, Linda A. Livingstone, and Lindos Daou

5 Entrepreneurs in Development: Vectors for Society's Progress 67
Taïeb Hafsi

6 **Redefining Corporate Social Responsibility** 81
Georges Azzi and Nehme Azoury

7 **The Impact of Businesses in the MENA Region** 91
Thami Ghorfi and Imad Eddine Hatimi

8 **Corporate Social Responsibility and Culture** 127
Jacques Rojot

9 **Middle Eastern Women in the Workplace: Between Traditional Careers and Entrepreneurship** 149
Madonna Salameh-Ayanian and Ursula El Hage

10 **Ethical and Political Marketing in the Middle East** 165
Charbel Salloum and Mario Sassine

Conclusion 179

Index 183

List of Figures

Fig. 3.1	Pie chart representing the nationality respondents	37
Fig. 3.2	Pie chart representing the range of industrial sectors of respondents	37
Fig. 3.3	Number of times each concept related to a distinct 'Gulf Arab leadership style' is mentioned	39
Fig. 3.4	Number of times each determinant of a distinct '*Gulf Arab leadership style*' is mentioned	42
Fig. 4.1	Trends for literacy for youth rates	52
Fig. 4.2	Unemployment rates by country	54
Fig. 4.3	Educational attainment of the population aged 25 years and older.	56
Fig. 4.4	Public investment in education in MENA countries (percentage of GDP)	58
Fig. 4.5	Life expectancy at birth	61
Fig. 6.1	Corporate Social Responsibility Pyramid	85
Fig. 7.1	The Evolution of the GDP growth rate in the MENA region	93
Fig. 7.2	The evolution of expenses related to health services	100
Fig. 7.3	Demographic evolution until 2050 in the MENA region	101
Fig. 7.4	The evolution of the GDP per capita in Morocco	103
Fig. 7.5	The evolution of the human development index in Morocco	103

Fig. 7.6 The evolution of the private capital contribution percentage to national investments in Morocco 104
Fig. 7.7 The evolution of the growth rates of the non-agricultural sector (OECD (2016)) 105
Fig. 7.8 The percentage of enterprises with R&D units in Morocco, according to their nature 109
Fig. 7.9 The evolution of Moroccan exports of transformed agri-food products 112
Fig. 7.10 The evolution of Morocco's exports structure between 1998 and 2004 115
Fig. 7.11 Implantation of Moroccan companies at the African level 117
Fig. 9.1 Career path linking "Aspiration" to the "Marital & Familial Status" of women 157

List of Tables

Table 3.1	Groups MOST likely to think there was a distinctive Gulf leadership style	38
Table 3.2	Groups LEAST likely to think there was a distinctive Gulf leadership style	38
Table 3.3	Inter-coder reliability test results	40
Table 3.4	Inter-coder reliability test results 2	40
Table 4.1	Trends for illiteracy for females	60
Table 7.1	Key conflict statistics for countries profiled, 2014	97

Introduction

With the development of globalization, communication and technology, businesses nowadays have grown to be an integral part of society. Business leaders are no longer regarded as leaders of their own businesses but leaders within society. Thus they often establish strong bonds and relationships with members of society while taking into account cultural, social, political, legal and economic aspects of their environment. This means that philanthropic initiatives are very different from the sustainable actions of day-to-day operations. With this in mind, this book aims to shed light on the concept of responsible business practice, considered a building block in the business context for the twenty-first century.

Countries that belong to the same region may share common ground in terms of territory, cultural practices and ethnic affiliation. However, at the same time, varieties in cultural, religious and traditional aspects of the society give rise both to diversity and homogeneity. This paradoxical effect is concretized through the common problems existing in the Mediterranean region and the challenges which are faced by organizations and people in this area. Thus, populations in the countries surrounding the Mediterranean Sea have developed over the years a strong character that is based on negotiation, trade and commerce. Furthermore, the history of the Mediterranean region stems from the interaction of the cultures and inhabitants around the coast—transport, trade and cultural exchange between diverse people that encompasses three continents:

Western Asia, North Africa and Southern Europe. It is also a cradle for three religions: Christianity, Islam and Judaism.

Therefore, in the business world companies' actions and their impact on society are very strongly related. The human aspect that encompasses all business practices has become a priority. In this context, we recall Albert Einstein's saying that: "All that is valuable in human society depends upon the opportunity for development accorded the individual."

Amidst all the political unrest and tragic events that are tarnishing the image and profile of the region, we still believe that we can remain true to our beliefs and values, striving for a better and more modern society. Societies that have passed through similar travails have reached a new beginning.

It is from this premise that we propose to discuss the unique blend between societies and businesses in the Mediterranean region. This book gathers together the work of public figures and academics from Middle Eastern and Arab society as well as from North America and Europe. This blend of expertise and knowledge will focus on the most common business practices in in relation to their effect on society in the Mediterranean countries.

The contributions will focus on these themes:

- Challenges and Opportunities for Contemporary Middle Eastern Society
- Businesses and Organizations for Sustainable Societies
- Culture and Business Operations: How Gulf Arab Leadership Style Impacts a Contingent Human Resource Management
- Development of Education and its Impact on Middle Eastern Societies
- Entrepreneurs in Development: Vectors for Society's Progress
- Redefining Corporate Social Responsibility
- The Impact of Businesses in the MENA (Middle East and North Africa) region
- Culture and Corporate Social Responsibility

Both contemporary and authentic in its tone and academic rigour, this book delves into a topic that has previously not been explored in such detail. In so doing, it creates a bridge between the business world on one side and modern Mediterranean society on the other.

USEK School of Business, Holy Spirit University of Kaslik, Jounieh, Lebanon

Nehme Azoury
USEK School of Business
Holy Spirit University of Kaslik
Jounieh, Lebanon

1

The Key Role of Media and Businesses in Helping Regional Societies Navigate Modern-Day Storms

Ramsay Najjar

The Pressing Need for Social Renewal (Introduction)

Dieter Helm, a British economist, once said that "there was enough oil in the world to fry the planet many times over." We might not be using the oil literally for this purpose, but we are definitely frying the planet on many levels, if we are to take into account the current threats to modern civilization. From climate change to religious fundamentalism, geopolitical mayhem, and overpopulation, and from environmental degradation to constrained resources and uncurbed consumerism, the world is facing unprecedented challenges on many fronts.

As it remains exposed to Western winds and local storms, continuously shaken by countless crises, the region has its own set of challenges. With high unemployment rates and growing extremism, declining standards

R. Najjar (✉)
Strategic Communication Consultancy, Beirut, Lebanon

N. Azoury (ed.), *Business and Society in the Middle East*,
DOI 10.1007/978-3-319-48857-8_1

of living, and a disconcerted youth, the region faces profound challenges for the years to come.

It is within this context of relatively weak political and social structures that Middle Eastern societies are left disoriented in the midst of it all. The region is in dire need of change, a sort of political, economic, and social renewal.

Considering the rather feeble governmental provision that prevails across the region, students, academics, lawyers, and activists, among others, have often taken up an active role in addressing environmental and social issues, with the burden of alleviating the needs of society more often than not relegated to non-governmental organizations (NGOs).

However, the undertakings of NGOs face their own set of challenges, especially when it comes to the extent and impact of the efforts made, the lack of oversight and regulation, as well as the unsustainable sources of funding for their organizations and initiatives.

Without disputing the model at hand, and irrespective of their best intentions, we have to concede that NGOs cannot do it alone. The ethical duty to address social and environmental challenges cannot be left just to them. When it comes to our part of the world, we have yet to fully recognize the crucial role that businesses could play in mitigating the risks to the environment they thrive in.

One need not be a devoted advocate of environmental preservation or social well-being to understand that, as individuals who live alongside businesses, the latter's activities and undertakings directly and indirectly affect our own.

While a business cannot fix it all either, it cannot shy away from addressing the challenges around it. Recognizing the reality that businesses cannot succeed if society fails, businesses can contribute to solving some of the social and environmental problems of our society and of our time.

Corporate Social Responsibility: A Wobbly Surge

The extent and nature of the involvement of the region's businesses in social affairs has primarily been through corporate social responsibility (CSR). However, such initiatives have yet to come of age, as they have mostly been tactical rather than strategic in their approach.

In fact, businesses have dabbled in CSR activities that have mostly been limited to the sponsoring of local events, the giving away of products, the broadcasting of punctual campaigns, the generation of biased and self-congratulatory reports, and others. These initiatives comprise in essence a myriad of feel-good projects that have been primarily used as public relations or communications tools rather than sustainable development opportunities. While they are a step in the right direction, none of them is effectively sustainable or impactful on the long term.

If one looks more closely at companies' initiatives, one notices that, when it comes to environmental responsibility, for example, there is often more talk than actual delivery. In fact, some companies can be accused of greenwashing, or using marketing and public relations gimmicks to make deceptive claims concerning their environmental responsibility. A simple yet common example of greenwashing is that of businesses who claim to have saved 10 percent of energy when in fact the drop was due to lower air-conditioning consumption that resulted from cooler weather conditions compared with previous years.

In the region, the banking sector is perceived as the most "advanced" in terms of CSR efforts. In fact, banks' social or environmental contributions go back a long way, well before the term CSR was even coined. Over the past decades, the local banking sector has increasingly embraced social responsibility and has launched several initiatives in this regard, including the sponsorship of cultural events, initiating some environmental projects, allocating resources to social causes, and others. However, the veracity and real impact of these efforts varies and has yet to be fully proven.

In Lebanon, for example, while the Central Bank has launched several circulars that favor CSR initiatives, the banking sector remains somewhat unregulated in this regard, leaving CSR undertakings and reporting at the discretion of the banks.

As such, it is not uncommon for the public to be subjected to a widespread campaign that promotes a bank's pledge to the environment, whereas this same bank lacks the simplest scheme of recycling paper in its offices and branches.

A deeper look at the way CSR is structured within banks leaves us to conclude that there is huge room for improvement, as only a handful of local banks boast an independent division dedicated to CSR. In fact, the latter is still part of the prerogatives of the communication and marketing departments, which suggests that social responsibility remains a communication tool rather than an integral part of the business's strategy.

In the real estate sector, for instance, there is a clear emergence of "green" construction in the region, with the growing knowledge, understanding, and expertise of green materials, processes, and equipment. This is the result of an increasingly conscious community and an easier access to international sources of green products. Effectively, significant strides have been made across the Gulf Cooperation Council (GCC) countries to promote water and energy efficiency, with local authorities working towards implementing regulations and rating systems that set higher standards for development and construction projects.

The truth of the matter is that, beyond overzealous public relations claims, it is important to ensure that businesses in general actually take a step back and reflect on the concrete role and responsibilities they have with regard to the ecosystem and society in which they operate.

The repercussions of image laundering or communicating about responsibility and actually doing little about it can be grave. When discovered, it is a challenging and consuming crisis to recover from. A recent example is Volkswagen's emissions rigging scandal that was extensively covered by the media, with clear hints as to the ridiculous aspect of the situation considering the fact that the company has been rated first on the Dow Jones Sustainability Index.

As such, it is important to recognize that a different approach to communication is needed, one that is based on concrete actions and genuine coverage rather than on initiatives that act as a front or as one-off undertakings that have form but no substance.

In a world of ambiguity and change, the main challenge for businesses is to cultivate public goodwill, and build and sustain a trusted and consistent image of their brand, one that is not made of smoke or a house of cards, but rather is based on solid foundations and deep roots. Knowing one's audience as well as their expectations is crucial. Violating these expectations can have substantial consequences on businesses' reputations, which can be irreversibly damaged or at least profoundly scarred. In fact, business ethics are increasingly becoming a make-or-break element of corporate reputation and image.

All in all, CSR should not be considered as an optional add-on that is external to core business operations. In fact, CSR should be integrated at strategy level, and businesses need to transform the way they function, integrating sustainability into all layers of business operations. So how can companies effectively harness these opportunities?

Businesses' Role in Weathering Social and Environmental Storms

Businesses should genuinely take part in the social conversation, bringing in new voices and creating value for society at large.

- Commitment at the Core

Concretely, businesses should start looking into investing money and expertise in strategic plans with the goal of improving the communities around them and taking a public stance when needed. As such, companies should rethink their strategies, revisit their social, environmental, or ethical commitments, and align them to the values that make up the core of their business.

For stakeholders and the public at large to engage and believe in companies' endeavors, it is important that they do not dilute their communication efforts but rather focus on one key issue or on interconnected issues. This could allow the business to win big in terms of brand enhancement and overall reputation as it takes ownership of a specific issue and humanizes the business by linking its name to positive initiatives.

A notable example is that of Continental, a German automotive manufacturing company that recently partnered with Welthungerhilfe, an organization for development and humanitarian aid, and the German Federal Employment Agency to establish a program that would enable refugees to enter the labor force more easily. This highlights an underlying trend, that of switching to communication that is geared towards meaning and actions (Continental 2015).

Looking at the region under consideration, which boasts increasingly high unemployment rates, estimated to be at 30 percent among the youth, businesses have a great opportunity to nurture future generations. Companies can tie their business strategies to their social commitments and involve themselves at a strategic level by participating in the educational path of the region's youth. Through providing targeted trainings and resources to students and helping them develop market-applicable skills, businesses can contribute to society while making sure there is a talented pool of youth with skills that they can tap into.

By engaging in a genuine effort to employ youth, businesses would enjoy fresh opportunities to increase their level of recognition and credibility among this target audience and beyond.

- Stakeholder Engagement

As important as it is to engage their own employees, businesses should also strive to engage all of their external stakeholders, ranging from their suppliers to their distributors, partners, consumers, and others. The best form of engagement is one that is holistic, takes into account each stakeholder's perceptions, and addresses their expectations. It is crucial for companies to ensure that proper communication and operational frameworks are set in place. This entails evaluating the impact of the business, setting public targets for improvements, and communicating around them. It is crucially important to communicate on the real and measurable progress so as to keep stakeholders engaged and interested in the company's enterprises. This emphasizes the need to craft a comprehensive strategic communication plan that helps stakeholders understand the long-term value of such initiatives.

For instance, Novartis, a pharmaceutical company, has gone a long way in integrating such principles. Its commitment to helping the underprivileged was manifested through giving away its drugs. As there was an evident limit to the quantity of drugs a company could distribute for nothing, it had to rethink the way in which it contributed to this target group. After spending considerable time listening to their needs and then working with its various stakeholders to fulfill them, Novartis rethought the distribution, packaging, and marketing of its drugs and now offers widely available low-cost drugs that benefit its target audience as well as the company's bottom line. By rethinking its strategy, Novartis succeeded in venturing into a new market while addressing, over the long term rather than a shorter period, an imperative social need: that of access to treatment.

On the local scene, a leading bank partnered with a local NGO through a volunteering program that entailed employees sharing their financial expertise to help the NGO better achieve its objectives. This kind of partnership could be extended to a broader array of skills and across several industries, whereby employers would encourage their employees to "'lend" their skills and put them at the service of the community. A media, communications, or advertising company could for instance provide employee volunteers who would contribute their communication expertise to help a nonprofit build its capacity and its reach. Other examples would be an engineering company lending its waste management expertise to help schools better manage their waste, a nutrition company sharing its knowledge and frameworks to institute healthy eating habits in schools, and an agribusiness company aiding local small-scale farmers with the handling of their crops. The opportunities are endless for companies to leverage their unique strengths and skill sets to enhance the abilities of the communities around them, in order to help them attain certain objectives or solve complex problems they may face. As the skills needed by civil society and the community are varied and plentiful, any company can partake in such an initiative, regardless of its size or of the industry in which it operates. These initiatives strive to strengthen the feel of inclusion, empower the employees, and consolidate the company's values.

- A Genuine and Transparent Narrative

As communication becomes an integral part of any business' success, it is important to do so in a way that engages stakeholders via a strong and authentic narrative. Maintaining a high level of transparency in all communication and leveraging the power of storytelling is critical, as is fashioning a strategy meant to build trust with the consumer base in the long term.

In fact, as consumer expectations are becoming increasingly demanding, and as the public becomes more skeptical of brands, it is crucial for businesses to demonstrate impact using a simplified, genuine, and relatable language, trimming the brand's message to the core. This will ensure that audiences properly understand the issues at hand and the concrete ways through which the business is addressing them.

In addition, collecting data, knowing how to use it, and presenting it to the public is essential work. For example, Nike, whose brand succeeded to a certain extent to overcome the perception that resulted from the child labor scandal of the '90s, dedicated a beautifully designed site to its CSR activities, featuring interactive visual data as well as compelling content regarding the company's sustainable innovations.

On the local scene, amidst the general confusion that usually surrounds contentious topics, and taking into account the somewhat limited discernment of audiences, businesses can stand out and palliate the need for clear and lucid information by acting as experts on the subject at hand. A business can showcase and reinforce its know-how, proficiency, and expertise through a myriad of activities that would help elevate the company's standing. Instead of simply disseminating messages about the company's capabilities through push communication and advertising, a business can provide content that is of value to its stakeholders and the community as a whole. While the platforms and mediums used to relay the content are certainly of importance, the main focus should be on the content itself, whereby companies should aspire to create a coherent and original narrative that resonates with its audience. A dairy company could, for example, take on an educational role and position itself as a nutritional expert by conducting studies and publishing reports on the local population's intake of vitamins and nutrients. It could expand on the benefits of healthy nutrition and showcase through recipes and interactive videos the ways in which individuals can incorporate them into their lifestyle. It could also venture beyond its product offering and address the importance of exercising on a regular basis. Regardless of the initiatives, a strategic narrative should be meticulously crafted around the business' activities in order to create a sense of cohesion and genuine appeal.

Businesses can also embrace the power of visuals and graphics to craft visually appealing content that mixes educational and entertainment dimensions and relays core messages in a manner that is accessible and of interest to target audiences.

In fact, a thoroughly thought-out content strategy goes a long way towards engaging consumers. Businesses should look into giving priority to content, disclosing strong and innovative ideas that stay far from the canned advertising messages that are centered on the company rather than on the consumer (Inc. Staff 2011).

- Communication Synergy

A company's discourse cannot be dissociated from its tangible undertakings, as a business should embody what it communicates. In this regard, a company's processes, policies, and procedures should reflect its outreach efforts: its vision, mission, values, and ethical standards should translate into concrete operational measures. In simple terms, businesses should "walk the talk."

Furthermore, to ensure the effective delivery of their key messages, businesses need to thoroughly think about the vehicles and platforms they use and understand their audiences and the most optimal mediums to reach them. With the digitization of media, and as e-reputation and online influence gains tremendous ground in the region, this includes making good use of social media and having a coherent presence online. That said, in an attempt to reach a wider audience, businesses should not forget the direct community in which they operate and work towards nurturing their relationships via town-hall meetings and local partnerships. What is key is to offer a certain complementarity and synergy between the online and offline.

Netflix, for instance, succeeded in walking the talk. The company announced that it will offer unlimited paid maternity and paternity leave for both birth and adoption during the first year. This announcement received a lot of praise for its generous and equal approach, especially considering that these new policies match what Netflix had been advocating in its communication. More so, the company even applies to a certain extent this concept of gender parity in the TV series it produces, ensuring an overall synergy in its communication messages (McCord 2014).

Human capital is vital to every business, and in a region where the ratio of women to men is substantial, it is long overdue that women are provided with the same career opportunities as men. Some local businesses have jumped on the bandwagon, launching focused communication that touches on women's place in the workplace and society as well as the related challenges and opportunities. Taking an effective and constructive step further would be for local businesses to proactively communicate their goal of achieving gender parity in their workplace and actually provide concrete opportunities for women advancement rather than solely talking about it (Harvard Business Review 2013).

All in all, it is important for businesses to be part of the debate that surrounds them and their environment, continuously communicating around it and consistently repeating their key messages.

Associated Rewards and Risks

The rewards in terms of brand reputation and value are immense for companies that genuinely align their business models and investment strategies with the bold solutions needed to ensure a sustainable economy, environment, and in turn society. In fact, the advantages of doing so are manifold, as positive outcomes of responsible business practices lead to greater competitive advantage, higher brand value, and enhanced brand reputation. Notwithstanding the amplified media coverage that would ensue and the considerable returns in terms of equity, businesses will benefit from increased stakeholder trust, who would be more likely to lend their long-term support and even brand advocacy. It ensures higher attraction and engagement of employees as well as better internal and external collaboration.

Not taking part in these changes could be harmful for a company's reputation, especially considering the power that now lies in people's hands with the advancement of technology and new media.

The case of Unilever serves to illustrate this emerging social power. In 2001, the company's thermometer assembly plant in India was shut down for violating environmental norms by discharging tons of mercury into the environment and impacting forests, groundwater, and the health of former employees. While legal action against the company had left it unpunished, it took one single rap video produced by a local artist 14 years later to draw more than 3.6 million views from around the world, gathering the support of the global online community and shedding light on the company's mercury legacy. The initiative took such proportions that the multinational giant was forced to take concrete action and compensate 591 former employees (Mackey 2015).

The Media's Role in Weathering Current and Upcoming Social Storms

As an entrenched part of the social fabric, affecting society inasmuch as it is affected by it, the media has a considerable role to play. In fact, it could be a much-needed catalyzer and powerful actor in this important conversation. This applies to both new media, which has made big strides in the region, as well as traditional media, which still maintains its weight.

- Encourage Businesses

First off, the media should trace the path for businesses to follow. It could provide extensive coverage of green and social investments so as to reward businesses and encourage others to take part. A rating system could also be created, one that quantifies social impact and assesses businesses according to their impact on communities, employees, consumers, and the environment, among others. Furthermore, and as a mean to recognize some of the companies' current efforts in terms of CSR, the media could institute awards that would reward best practices and incentivize other businesses to follow suit. Media outlets could even partner with both the public and private sector to materialize efforts in this direction.

- Act as Watchdogs

The media could also embrace its noble role as fourth estate and watchdog by exposing the hollowness of CSR initiatives and highlighting deceptive campaigns that create the illusion of responsibility. Greenwashing, fake labels, and image laundering are all prevalent communication tactics that are used throughout the region, and indeed the world. These tactics are aimed at deceiving consumers and could certainly be curbed by the media.

The media could address a number of prevailing malpractices that are undertaken by businesses across industries. A flagrant area to look into is one that is related to consumers' health and safety, whether linked to, for example, food, medication, treatment, and hospitalization. Locally, different sectors have been shaken by scandals related to the health and safety of society, including counterfeit medications, shady practices, unregulated sales, food contamination and non-compliance, and so on, which are areas in which the media could play a critical role in exposing the venality of businesses involved in such practices, especially in a country with deficient laws, limited liability, and semi-absent accountability.

- Preemptively Immunize

The role of the media does not stop there. In fact, the media should be emboldened to take up a more proactive role, one that creates awareness of critical issues and preempts them, before they turn into fully fledged crises to simply report on. The garbage crisis that has plagued Lebanon is a case in point. Rather than spotting the early signs leading to the degradation of the situation, the media could have played a role in sounding the alarm a long time ago. Through proper investigative journalism and coverage of government and business failings concerning waste management and sustainable disposable and treatment of trash, the media could have raised the issue, forcing it into the court of public opinion and instigating concerned parties to act before the situation became overwhelmingly disastrous.

As such, the media could further use its means and resources to create a sense of urgency for businesses to become more responsible and to weave sustainable environmental and social practices into their core business practices. The media could also engage businesses in debate and help them understand the benefits associated with integrating social and environmental aspects in their business models.

- Educate Audiences

The aforementioned preemptive and preventive efforts would naturally ensue from a deeper awareness of the prevailing issues, hence the media's crucial role in raising awareness, educating citizens, and helping change their mindsets.

Most notably, the media should help draw people's attention to the environmental and social practices of businesses. More media coverage and airtime could be provided for experts as well as pilot projects in an attempt to expand the knowledge and confidence of the different stakeholders, be they consumers, businesses, or authorities, for example.

For instance, as gender parity is a growing topic in the region, the media can have a say in the general discourse by normalizing the idea of women taking leading positions through their gender-balanced reporting. One example of a way in which journalists could play their part is by purposefully and mindfully varying their sources and quoting female business leaders, giving them the same attention that is given to their male counterparts.

Furthermore, consumer education is key, as the reality at hand is that more often than not, the public is not capable of differentiating between genuine initiatives and those that are not. In light of the today's regional political and social context, the media could take it upon itself to emphasize the individual and active role that citizens could play in society and shed light on the duties and responsibilities of all players. More so, the media could help society grasp that in the bigger scheme of things all members are intertwined, and that each decision, whether it emanates from a political leader or a business owner, affects them directly or indirectly. These efforts could be manifested through impactful and educational yet entertaining content that instills a sense of citizenship and elucidates concepts that remain foreign, such as accountability, transparency, governance, and more.

In effect, by highlighting the implications of having businesses behave responsibly, the media would be able to garner and leverage the needed voices to hold businesses accountable and effect real change.

- Influence Key Powers

Media outlets could certainly go beyond this, and pressure legislative powers and concerned parties to introduce reforms and policies that regulate and reward sustainable business practices. An example is rethinking the tax policy and awarding tax breaks to eligible businesses, hence encouraging and rewarding sustainable practices.

Furthermore, most countries in the region do not have the legal frameworks that regulate CSR. As such, the media could also push for the adoption of related legal frameworks similar to France's Grenelle I and II laws.

It is a fact that some businesses and media outlets in the region are already doing some of the above, joining forces to institute change. It is up to the public to push and encourage the media to go even further and deeper in this direction. There are nonetheless some big challenges ahead. In order to ensure the seemly evolution of society, the predominant barrier to be broken remains free and independent access to information for all. In fact, one needs to acknowledge that the current standing of traditional media is far from optimal, considering the sturdy political grip over media independence. Furthermore, Internet metrics remain extremely low in the region and in comparison to the rest of the world. If society is to challenge the status quo, there is an imperative need to secure a more extensive and performing access to the Internet, thus giving society the tools and resources to voice its concerns and expectations, and as such affect businesses inasmuch as they affect society (Lubber 2016).

The Imperative Need for Change (Conclusion)

Whether seen as a response to business risks or as an ethical duty, corporate and media responsibility with regard to social and environmental challenges is necessary. This is not an undertaking that can be achieved quickly, but because of its nature and urgency, it is a process that will have a long-lasting impact.

A recent global study conducted by APCO Worldwide stated that 94 percent of those surveyed agreed that companies are able to shape a better society. According to the *Harvard Business Review*, millennials, who make up roughly 50 percent of the global workforce, stated that they are looking for work that connects to a larger purpose. In fact, younger generations are striving to lead the way in redefining success in business and considering new measures in the equation such as social and environmental dimensions (Bresman 2015).

By introspecting about its own capabilities, anticipating society's needs and addressing them through responsible practices, it is up to the current generation of businesses to transform their operations and models so as to resonate with today's employees and consumers. When zooming in on the region, one need not look too far to unearth opportunities for betterment. It has become evident that the region is in dire need of massive governmental restructuring and renewal of legislations and policies. However, we do not need to wait for that to happen in order to institute change. As new missions and values make their way through the business community, and as sustainable best practices powered with genuine communication become the new norm, one can aspire to a better tomorrow. With the devastating loss of trust in governments, we can work to vaccinate the region's businesses and empower them to become a beacon of hope and a safe harbor in the midst of all the storms.

Bibliography

Bresman, H. (2015, February). What millennials want from work. *Harvard Business Review*. Retrieved from https://hbr.org/2015/02/what-millennials-want-from-work-charted-across-the-world&cm_sp=Article-_-Links-_-End%20of%20Page%20Recirculation

Continental Donates €100,000 to Welthungerhilfe to Support Syrian Refugees. (2015, December). Retrieved from http://www.continental-corporation.com/www/pressportal_com_en/themes/press_releases/1_topics/work_life-en/donation-welthungerhilfe-en.html

Harvard Business Review. (2013, September). Women in the workplace: A research roundup. Retrieved from https://hbr.org/2013/09/women-in-the-workplace-a-research-roundup

Inc. Staff. (2011). How a business can change the world. *Inc. Magazine*. Retrieved from http://www.inc.com/magazine/20110501/how-a-business-can-change-the-world.html

Lubber, M. S. (2016). Business as the engine of social change. *McKinsey Voices on Society*. Retrieved from http://voices.mckinseyonsociety.com/business-as-the-engine-for-social-change/#sthash.9q8Hvbd1.dpuf

Mackey, R. (2015, July). Indian rapper calls out unilever to a Nicki Minaj beat. *The New York Times*. Retrieved from http://www.nytimes.com/2015/08/01/world/asia/indian-rapper-calls-out-unilever-to-a-nicki-minaj-beat.html?_r=0

McCord, P. (2014, January). How netflix reinvented HR. *Harvard Business Review*. Retrieved from https://hbr.org/2014/01/how-netflix-reinvented-hr

2

Business and Organization for Sustainable Societies

"Inclusiveness in the Arab Region: A Necessity or a Luxury?"

Karim Seghir

Introduction

The concept of "business" has long been at the core of civilization. Starting off with the very basic rules of negotiation and trade, this concept has rapidly evolved to mean so much more. Businesses no longer have the elementary purpose of commercial activity merely to buy and sell—they now have a *responsibility* to the communities and people around them. There has been a growing trend around the terms *sustainability* and *inclusivity*, to which many businesses have responded. More and more corporations are looking into how they can participate in sustainability issues and integrate them with their strategies.

This is especially true when we look at businesses in developing areas, such as the Arab region. Looking back thousands of years, there was always a connection between the business sector and its surrounding

K. Seghir (✉)
American University of Cairo (AUC), Cairo, Egypt

N. Azoury (ed.), *Business and Society in the Middle East*,
DOI 10.1007/978-3-319-48857-8_2

society there. The development of trade and commerce served as a link between North Africa, Asia, and the Levant. It created a bond between different cultures, allowing people to explore and increase their knowledge. The Arabic language itself, a member of the Semitic family, was created through this mixing of civilizations.

Arab societies continued to thrive in the business sector and rise to the top, and until today this region is characterized by the high number of businesses and organizations. However, the focus remains on traditional economic measures such as gross domestic product (GDP) growth, foreign direct investment (FDI), and the competitiveness index when this is misleading and not sustainable. If the recent popular uprisings in the Arab region have taught us one thing, it is that in an environment that focuses solely on maximizing shareholders' value, we should not expect individuals to care about sustainability, poverty, corruption, equality, and the other chronic socioeconomic challenges the region is facing. In fact, most countries that experienced the Arab Spring had good economic growth according to traditional economic measures prior to the uprisings; but the growth was exclusive.

Achieving inclusiveness requires much more than just looking at economic factors—it requires businesses to help find solutions to societal problems and integrate them within their strategies. It requires individuals who are responsible and innovative to create better dialogue between business and society, to bridge this gap, and to ensure the ideas, knowledge, and perspectives of citizens are being heard. This is why economic growth is not the right measure when it comes to understanding business in society, especially in the Arab region. By focusing on the inclusivity of women, youth, and all other members of the society, we will be able to achieve a sustainable future. Achieving an inclusive and sustainable future can only be accomplished if we encourage public, private, and non-governmental sectors to be responsible for the community, in addition to seeking profit.

Likewise, business schools in the Arab region should assume their key mission in fostering an inclusive and sustainable society by graduating responsible leaders and professionals who will create lasting values and drive change on a global scale. Aside from empowering women and youth, securing a living income for all through supporting small and medium-size businesses and enhancing the quality of corporate social responsibility (CSR), ensuring quality of education, health services, and housing facilities for all are also major aspects that can connect together the bigger picture for incorporating sustainability and inclusivity to all sectors of society.

The purpose of this chapter is to express the author's views not only as the Dean of the American University in Cairo (AUC) School of Business, but also as a citizen of the Arab region who strongly believes in its huge potential. The theme of sustainability and inclusivity for all social sections has always been an important topic, and will be examined throughout this chapter by looking at the current situation of business in the Arab region, by discussing what the AUC School of Business has been doing to promote this theme, expressing the views and goals for the future of business in Arab societies, and finally by suggesting strategies for targeting any future challenges. The impactful offering and initiatives that will be shared here have been recognized by the most prominent accrediting and ranking agencies in the world, such as the European Quality Improvement System (EQUIS), the Association to Advance Collegiate Schools of Business (AACSB), the Association of MBAs (AMBA), Eduniversal, Five-Palmes League of Excellence, and the *Financial Times*.

The AUC School of Business as a Promoter of Inclusivity and Sustainability

For about seven decades, the AUC School of Business has witnessed and withstood numerous environmental changes that have shaped its philosophy to meet the needs and challenges of an ever-changing business education. The School's vision is to be the leading knowledge hub with Arab region relevance and global influence, while its mission is to develop entrepreneurial and responsible global leaders and professionals. The emphasis of the vision and the mission is to continue to be a global institution with deeply rooted regional expertise and impact. The School focuses on three strategic themes: Entrepreneurship/family business, responsible business, and economic development. These themes are also key topics in the Arab region, providing even more reason for their importance. The School's core values lie in a sense of belonging and pride for both the School and region, ambition and a desire to stretch the horizon by charting new and untapped opportunities, integrity and good citizenship, and a sense of excellence and urge for continuous advancement, improvement and intellectual growth.

Academics alone, however, cannot fully promote sustainability and inclusivity, which is why the School has a variety of research centers and programs which will be discussed later on, specializing in entrepreneurship, philanthropy, civic leadership, responsible business, economic development, and more.

Description of the Current Situation

The Arab region has a long history of running businesses and basing its society on business culture. This has continued up until current times, and has grown even more. Over 64% of working age individuals in this region would rather start their own businesses than work for a company as an employer. Within the past five years, around 70% of individuals have actually taken the initiative towards establishing their own businesses in the region. This means that entrepreneurship levels have been raised drastically over the years, proving that citizens of this region have a strong urge to better their societies and have innovative ideas that deserve to be supported. Across the region more and more youth have been joining the business sphere as leaders. The 2016 rankings of MENA (Middle East and North Africa) countries in the Global Entrepreneurship Index listed UAE at number 19, Qatar at 24, Saudi Arabia at 36, Lebanon at 50, Morocco at 78, and Egypt at a staggering 89.

In the Arab region, many businesses and organizations have begun incorporating sustainability and inclusivity in order to better bond with the wider society. In Egypt, a country with a population of around 85 million people, the Arab Spring brought with it many economic disruptions which are still present today. Government intervention has made it difficult for organizations and firms to obtain licenses and formally operate. Corruption and greed have caused a majority of the population not to trust the government or any official authorities. Paying taxes is a recurring problem, as people simply do not believe their hard-earned money will be used properly. With small and medium-size businesses employing almost three-quarters of the nation's labor force and accounting for 63% of its GDP, this negative attitude which clouds the country needs to be removed.

Around 29% of total employment in Egypt is in the public sector, almost double the world average rate. As mentioned previously, the government must work together with private, public, and non-profit sectors to create a harmonious business culture which will in turn benefit everyone and avoid an economic crisis. This is difficult, however, when each sector views the other through its own lens, ignoring the benefits each has to offer. The government sees the private sector as a "cash cow" and civil society as a burden, while the private sector views the public as a burden and civil society as unskilled, and in turn civil society views the government as a corrupt entity working for itself and the private sector as crooks with nothing but greed and profit in their agendas. With this mindset, how can we ever expect to have a prosperous future? The unfortunate thing is that citizens, among them our youth, are caught in this cross-fire.

In several Arab countries, the government is perceived by many as more of a liability than an enabler. Empowering the private sector and creating more separation from the public sector is critical to unleashing the potential of the private sector to create growth. The lack of transparency is also a long-standing problem, which only feeds into the public's mistrust towards the government and other agencies. In order to move forward, we must establish a reliable framework of policies and regulations for doing business in the Arab region that must remain consistent with international norms, yet stays true to our unique culture. Promoting decentralization to empower local communities is also a necessity, as all parts of a society should be included if we are to move towards sustainability and inclusivity.

Working more with non-profit organizations is also crucial, as they can bridge the bond between business and society through their direct dealings with the community. By giving more aid to these organizations and including them in business school strategies, we can better hope to reach all members of the community and connect them with businesses to see how each side can help the another. If communities express their needs, businesses can move towards finding solutions to these issues, which would fall under their CSR units. A new addition to the business world, CSR has been catching on quickly in the Arab region; and in Egypt, several companies are now well known for their CSR projects.

An issue that this region faces in terms of CSR and sustainability in general, however, is that many of the elder generation businessmen and women remain tied to their traditional ideologies, refusing to conform to the changes of modern times. These traditional values remain focused on profits and expanding the business, with little to no emphasis on community and well-being. This is why the AUC School of Business uses a very practical approach to business education, rooted in a liberal arts educational context which aims to foster critical thinking, creativity, emotional intelligence, problem-solving skills, and a deep sense of responsibility towards society. If past generations cannot change their ways, then it is the responsibility of business schools to ensure we graduate innovative and responsible citizens who are forward-thinking in their goals and most importantly are able to adapt to changes. The AUC School of Business, therefore, is strongly focused on developing responsible leaders who can lead the Arab region into a prosperous future and make a transformative impact within their communities.

In forging this pathway for the future, business schools should aim at addressing contemporary issues of deeply rooted regional significance. One of the most pressing challenges the Arab region is currently facing is unemployment. With almost 3 million young people entering the job market in the region annually, a sustainable and viable solution to this rising challenge of unemployment is a well-directed entrepreneurship ecosystem. In 2010, AUC School of Business launched the Entrepreneurship and Innovation Program, which is mandated to educate citizens in the Arab region in entrepreneurship and to infuse them with the desire to create and innovate. The School is working on entrepreneurship in Africa as well as launching the African Academic Association on Entrepreneurship (AAAE), which includes six universities in Africa. AAAE is mandated to build linkages among African business schools focusing on teaching and research in the areas of entrepreneurship and family business.

In 2013, the Venture Lab (V-Lab), a business incubator, was launched under the School of Business as a way in which to directly impact young businesses within its surrounding community. V-Lab, the first university-based incubator in Egypt, translates technologies and innovations into commercially viable ventures, thereby contributing to economic development and job creation. The startups that join benefit from training and mentoring sessions, access to venture capitalists and angel investors, and are able to capitalize on AUC's intellectual capital, world-class facilities, and research capacities. Not only does this program help startups and the entrepreneurial community in Egypt, it also gives them the chance to give back and share their entrepreneurial experience with students and staff at AUC. Through this, it fosters a thriving ecosystem of innovation, education, and responsible business.

Despite it being a rather new program, V-Lab was recently recognized as one of the top five most promising university-based incubators in Africa by the Sweden-based UBI index—a notable honor and a strong indicator of AUC's commitment to helping the region's employment plight. Within a three-year span, V-Lab has completed six incubation cycles, incubated 50+ startups that raised $5 million in funding, produced $6 million in revenues, and created over 300 jobs.

The AUC and its School of Business cannot claim to support the community without giving special attention to its female members. Women's inequality is a pressing matter in the Arab region, and a topic the School takes very seriously. For this reason, we have initiated several programs focusing on empowering women to pursue their entrepreneurial goals. The first is the Women's Empowerment and Leadership Program, created in partnership with Wharton School of the University of Pennsylvania in 2008. Its commitment to enhancing the growth and development of women entrepreneurs in the Arab region through a unique blend of certificate programs, research programs, and mentoring and networking activities gives women the ability to lead the social and economic development of the region. So far, this program has graduated over 400 women entrepreneurs, and counting.

After the successful launch of this program, the School of Business partnered with Goldman Sachs that same year to create the Goldman Sachs 10,000 Women Entrepreneurship and Leadership Program, providing 10,000 women entrepreneurs from developing countries with an education in business and management. In 2015, the program launched its sixth cohort and partnered with Babson College, a world leader in entrepreneurship education, which developed a new global curriculum just for the program. The third initiative which the School of Business runs is called Women on Board. This aims to improve the gender balance of corporate boards in Egypt and the Arab region. It focuses on sensitizing male board members to gender issues, qualifying women from different corporate sectors and outside the corporate mainstream to be appointed to corporate boards, and advocating for policy and legislative changes that institutionalize gender diversity on corporate boards.

Another issue in inclusivity is that people in the Arab region lack the proper skillsets required by the job market. To support this issue, we have been offering a very large Executive Education operation since 1977, targeting relevant issues such as health care management, crisis management, risk management, real estate, logistics, family business, and much more. In August 2011, this received accreditation from the Accrediting Council for Education and Training (ACCET) for a five-year period. Through such programs, business schools can enable today's business leaders to develop the strategic thought processes and skills necessary to successfully grow their businesses in a dynamic and global marketplace. With a total of 5000 participants annually, it has reached an alumni count of 170,000 since its initiation, with regional programs spanning the region in Bahrain, Dubai, Jordan, Saudi Arabia, and Oman. These programs feature management curricula customized to the needs of managers and executives at all levels, working in global companies, government agencies, and non-profit organizations. By doing so, we are able to direct leaders and managers of these sectors towards paths of sustainability and inclusivity, and guide them towards working together harmoniously.

Driven by its mission to develop responsible leaders, the AUC School of Business became the Principles for Responsible Management Education (PRME) MENA Chapter Coordinator and an active member of prominent associations such as the Academy of Business in Society (ABIS), the Egyptian Corporate Responsibility Center, and the Bottom of the Pyramid Global Network.

There is no doubt that technology is key to the future, and business schools must work with it to remain relevant and more impactful with young generations. The Queen Rania Foundation for Education and Development, in partnership with EdX, launched Edraak, a not-for- profit platform that aims to develop MOOCs (massive open online courses) for the Arabic region (80% of which is not English speaking). It aims to present the Arab region with unique and vital opportunities which could help revolutionize education and learning. This program selects a group of regional universities, offering them more than 24 online courses in Arabic, and includes over 130,000 learners of which 40% are female. At AUC in particular, the courses offered as part of this program are Economic Development of the Arab Region, Entrepreneurship, and Responsible Business. To date, there are over 1 million users of this program, proving once again that the AUC School of Business offers its community cream of the crop opportunities and experiences.

With globalization being a key player in the world of sustainability and inclusivity, universities must have a regional impact in order to spread a sense of harmony and unity. Producing and disseminating knowledge about the Arab region's business environment is crucial in order to better work together, which is why the School launched the El-Khazindar Business Research and Case Center (KCC) in 2008 to produce and disseminate local business cases that provide business leaders with pertinent knowledge about challenges and opportunities specific to the Arab region. The KCC focuses on three main dimensions: practical publications, knowledge dissemination, and teaching enhancement.

Lack of civic engagement and social responsibility is another issue this region faces, however, the concept of philanthropy and being involved in one's community has been steadily increasing. In 2006, the John D. Gerhart Center for Philanthropy, Civic Engagement and Responsible Business was established to promote social change in the Arab region through building a culture of effective giving and civic responsibility. In addition to disseminating research and policy papers, the Center strives to build capacity for leadership among Arab youth and to enhance their ability to become more engaged in civic matters. Through fellowships such as the Lazord Academy, seminars, conferences, publications, and digital platforms, the center is filling important information gaps and providing analysis of trends and critical issues in the field.

Future Perspective

The future of incorporating sustainability and inclusivity in all sectors of society and tightening the relationship between society and business will greatly depend on how much responsibility corporations and business schools decide to take. As leaders in our communities, it is our job to act as mentors and influence those around us in a positive way. Private businesses and large corporations should strive to support their communities and surrounding society by expanding their CSR units and also improving the quality of life for their employees.

A backbone of the economy in the Arab region is family-owned businesses, which account for about 50% of private sector employment and more than 80% of the total companies in the region. Business schools in the Arab region should help business-owning families better understand and navigate challenges, such as governance, succession plans, and innovation and entrepreneurial spirit, which will in turn have a positive impact on companies' sustainability, longevity, and growth, and consequently assist in the creation of long-lasting jobs. AUC School of Business strives to foster the development of family-owned businesses in the Arab region by providing tailored services through a range of executive education programs, academic courses, case studies, round tables, and workshops.

Instilling regional perspectives as well as global ones is also a necessity in order to ensure sustainability and inclusivity in the region. Graduates need to have a strong sense of perspective concerning and knowledge of their region. Unfortunately, owing to the economic and political situation of the Arab region, many community members opt to travel abroad in order to pursue their careers. This is especially true for the younger generations. This, however, creates an unstable economy and an unclear future for the region, as we remain limited in our ability to retain fresh new minds. In this regard, the mission of business schools in our region should not focus on the education of their students according only to global trends, but also concerning geographic location. Going forward, business schools should address global trends while responsibly contributing to the pressing and chronic socioeconomic issues relevant to their region. Only by doing so can we hope to raise interest in our students, and thereby graduate citizens who are more willing and able to assist their own communities rather than seeking a career elsewhere.

Technology and online learning should also play a huge role in incorporating sustainability and inclusivity, as business schools around the region can easily link to businesses by building their corporate relations strategy around the recognition of the reciprocal nature of such relationships. Schools can therefore interact with corporations at different levels of engagement in all their activities. Initiatives to strengthen corporate connections include internship opportunities, inviting guest speakers from the corporate sector, customizing executive education programs, creating lifelong partnership with alumni that can enhance student experience and program value, and promoting practical research-related activities. Establishing an advisory board composed of leaders from the corporate sector is a good catalyst for strengthening corporate connections. In addition, strong corporate connections often lead to substantial fundraising opportunities such as endowed professors, fellowships and scholarships, research grants, and gifts to finance relevant and impactful initiatives. These connections are also important for business schools in understanding the needs of businesses so they can graduate students with the right skillsets; and maintain strong ties with alumni who are working in the corporate world, and as such can help build bridges between their alma mater and their workplaces. Effective corporate connections are also key for developing pertinent executive education programs that address the needs of businesses and ensure continuous dialogue with various sectors in the industry.

If we aim to promote inclusivity, then including other schools aside from business schools is a must. We should "practice what we preach." Including other schools such as humanities and social sciences would help produce a well-rounded understanding of the situation. If we are discussing how to connect business with society, both sides need to be part of the picture. Business schools must do their part in sharing their knowledge of the business world, just as humanities and social science schools should do. These schools can offer an insight into the nature of societies and how best to interact with communities and people.

Business schools in the Arab region should refrain from adopting a completely theoretical approach that focuses solely on functional areas. AUC School of Business uses a very practical approach to business education that is rooted in a liberal arts educational context which fosters critical thinking, creativity, emotional intelligence, and problem-solving skills. New and creative teaching methods whereby students are engaged and taught concepts through experiential learning and other means need to be used. Moreover, business schools in the region should work on bridging the gap between business education and the corporate sector in order to maximize their students' readiness to effectively join the business world.

The AUC prides itself in being a global university, with over 170,000 alumni having graduated from all their local and regional programs combined. The students come from diverse backgrounds, in terms of socioeconomic standing, gender, and nationality. In all, 75% of the students get financial aid, with 17% of the operating budget to cover students' scholarship. The LEAD program was created to offer scholarships to Thanaweya Amma students graduating with high grades, as a reward for their hard work.

Suggested Strategies for Targeting the Future Challenges

There are sure to be future challenges surrounding the concepts of sustainability and inclusivity in all social sectors, whether they come from the government, corporations, or society itself. However, as mentors and leaders in our community, it is our role as educational institutions to work together to overcome these challenges. In fact, finding solutions to these challenges could actually spark a movement for inclusivity and bonding between business and society, as we can reach out to different social sectors to listen to their ideas and suggested solutions. Using the values and mission of the AUC School of Business, graduating well-rounded, out of the box students who have critical and analytical thinking skills is the first step to fighting any challenges. Business schools must highlight a deep sense of responsibility towards society and citizenship in its students, as they will be shaping the future of their country and region. Providing support for our communities and business partners is another strategy that may be used in tackling challenges.

The rapid transformations that the world has been undergoing over the past decades and the changes in needs and skills of the new generation have led to a significant alteration in business education. Ten years from now, the needs, challenges, and opportunities of business education will have metamorphosed. Only innovative and agile business schools will survive and evolve, given the rapid market changes and the fierce competition. In such a fast-changing world, business schools must constantly revisit what to teach and how.

Business schools ought to use a very experiential approach both inside and outside the classroom. Furthermore, although the world is becoming more globalized than ever, local relevance remains vital. Business schools, especially in developing countries, should use a "glocalized" approach that addresses the specific needs and challenges of the region. In terms of teaching approaches, business schools must be innovative in catering to the needs and the skills of the new generation in a way that is technology-savvy and more risk-taking than the previous one. This includes cutting-edge teaching techniques, innovative and impactful research, and pertinent executive education programs.

Conclusion

The topic of businesses and societies for sustainable societies is very important in today's modern world. Giving back to the community and improving the well-being of employees and citizens around the world has been a growing trend, especially in the Arab region. Sparked by the Arab Spring, this sense of responsibility to others is one that the AUC School of Business instilled in its core values from day one. By graduating students intelligent in both academics and life experiences, our School can guarantee a bright future and relationships between business and society in the region and beyond.

It is the responsibility of our institutions to prepare the leaders of tomorrow who will convert such concepts into reality and to support research that can enhance our imagination and push the envelope for a fuller realization of a sustainable and inclusive society. The events of the revolution challenged traditional views on economic development and generated a pressing need to foster a fresh and innovative perspective on issues pertaining to economic growth, development, civic society, and sustainability to create an inclusive region where everyone has the opportunity to share the same benefits and sense of well-being. Given their distinct location and wealth of expertise on the Arab region, business schools have an unprecedented opportunity to contribute to the development of an emerging Arab economy founded on the principles of inclusiveness and accountability.

The AUC School of Business strives to provide its students not only with an international and diverse learning environment, but also with intelligence on regional matters in order to develop them into entrepreneurial and responsible global leaders and professionals who have a deep sense of responsibility towards their region. Management education must work hard on developing responsible business leaders by shifting the culture from one of pure market capitalism, profit maximization, and perpetual growth to one that upholds and values the role of business in society, sustainable development, and stakeholder interests. The impact of business schools instilling these values in their students will be seen when future leaders make ethical decisions that take into account multiple factors aside from profit, which will in turn benefit the community as a whole.

The number of life-changing innovations we have seen in the past few years is nothing less than unbelievable. There are countless ways to support one another; we just have to be open to seeing and understanding them. Once the link between society, businesses, and educational institutions is created, nothing can stop the Arab region from fulfilling its full potential and having the brightest future the world has yet to see.

3

Culture and Business Operations: How the Gulf Arab Leadership Style Impacts a Contingent Human Resource Management

William Scott-Jackson and Jonathan Michie

Introduction

This chapter reports the results of interviews with Gulf Arab corporate leaders that indicate a rather distinct Gulf 'leadership style', discusses the nature of this Gulf leadership style, and considers what implications it might have for various aspects of Human Resource Management (HRM) policies and practices. The leadership style of Gulf Arabs has not been widely studied, despite studies of Arab Leadership (Muna 1980) and Islamic Leadership (Beekun and Badawi 1999; Adair 2010). Some have examined leadership within a single Gulf Cooperation Council (GCC) country, such as Ismaily (2004) for Oman, or have included aspects of leadership as part of multi-regional comparative cultural studies such as the GLOBE study (House et al. 2002; Shi and Wang 2011) or the earlier

W. Scott-Jackson
Oxford Strategic Consulting, 34 St John St, Oxford, OX1 2LH, UK

J. Michie (✉)
Kellogg College, University of Oxford, Oxford, UK

N. Azoury (ed.), *Business and Society in the Middle East*,
DOI 10.1007/978-3-319-48857-8_3

work of Hofstede and Hofstede (2001) and Trompenaars and Hampden-Turner (1998). HRM in the GCC has received attention (Aycan et al. 2007; Budhwar and Mallahi 2006), but the implications for a contingent HRM in the GCC has not been researched previously.

The role of leadership has long been recognized as playing a crucial role in HRM systems and in corporate performance (Bass 1985; Day and Lord 1988). It is, of course, possible that any relationship between a leadership style and a contingent HRM may be due to causality in either direction, or indeed both may be due to an overarching variable, such as organizational or national culture. The chapter explores these issues as follows: 'The Literature' reports on the existing literature, 'Research Methods and Scope' discusses methods, 'Interviews with 50 Senior Corporate Leaders' reports our findings of a 'Gulf Arab leadership style', our findings regarding a contingent GCC HRM system are reported in 'Implications for HRM', and Section 6 concludes.

The Literature

While studies on the Gulf—or wider Arab—leadership style are scarce (Al Omian and Weir 2005), research on Arab culture (Allen et al. 2006), globalization, and the Arab world (Fox et al. 2006) is relevant, as are country-specific reviews such as Lacey (2009) on competing power models in the Kingdom of Saudi Arabia (KSA), Al Abed and Hellyer (2001) on tribal society and leadership in the United Arab Emirates (UAE), Fromherz (2012) on frameworks of authority in Qatar, Al Ismaily (2004) on Omani organizational culture, and Cummins (2012) on the political history of the Gulf States.

Research has tended to focus on describing the cultural and societal factors that determine particular elements of the Gulf, or most often superordinate approaches to leadership, such as 'Arab' (Muna 2003), 'Middle Eastern' (House et al. 2002), and 'Islamic' (Adair 2010). The former studies tend to utilize models of cultural difference (Trompenaars and Woolliams 2003) to suggest why, and in what ways, cultural differences impact behaviours, such as leadership and its components. The literature suggests that the major factors shaping a Gulf leadership style are as follows:

1. Ali (1990) suggests that one of the strongest influences on Arab culture, business practices, and leadership has been religion, specifically **Islam**. This influence includes a general concern for the spiritual aspects of life, where, for example, Nusair (1983) suggests adding 'spiritual fulfilment' to the Maslow (1943) hierarchy of needs. Adair (2010) stresses the role of the leader as both serving and leading, using the Prophet Mohammed's life as a role model. Some have suggested that the Quran provides guidance on leader behaviours: for example, Islam is a brotherhood where personal worth is not dictated by status and wealth (Kabasakal and Bodur 2002); Yousef (2001) found a positive relationship between the Islamic work ethic and organizational commitment, job satisfaction, and attitudes to change; and Whiteoak et al. (2006) found that the Islamic work ethic was a strongly held 'ideal' in the UAE.
2. Hofstede's early analysis, re-presented in Hofstede and Peterson (2000), and Kabasakal and Bodur's (2002) study both suggest that Arabic **culture** is relatively high on collectivism (where self-interest and work pressure is subordinate to the family/tribe and other relationships), and also high on power-distance (the degree to which the power of the most senior differs from that of subordinates). Kabasakal and Bodur (2002) note that the Arab 'cluster' is low on uncertainty avoidance, future orientation, and gender egalitarianism. Ali and Camp (1995) illustrate the main cultural differences between US and Arab cultures and the implications of these for management theory—confirming the importance of relationships over task, the desire to operate in a family structure with a strong father figure, and an avoidance of damaging conflict. Yasin and Stahl (1990) confirm that, in this affiliation-oriented culture, most managers would demonstrate a greater affiliation orientation than would effective managers in the high power/achievement cultures of the West.
3. Ali (1990) points out that structure, strategy, and organization in the Arab business are often predicated on **tribal and family factors**, rather than on pure business or market needs. Muna (1980) found that Arab executives maintain strong ties with extended families even if they are living abroad.

4. Much of the Arab world, including the GCC states, has been affected by European and Ottoman **colonial bureaucracies**: Ali (1990) suggests that this legacy includes a strict adherence to the chain of command, adherence to the scalar principle (communicating only through management layers), and centralized decision-making.
5. Over two decades ago, Ali (1990) noted that Arab attitudes to business and management were being impacted by **Western influence**, with an increasing awareness of waste and the misuse of resources, concern for the image of the organization, increased flexibility and pragmatism, a greater cognizance of the systems approach, and a tolerance for ambiguity and the demands of multiple roles. But Westernization is sometimes seen as corrupting, materialistic, weakening family values, and destroying the moral and social basis of society (Ayubi 1988).
6. Role models are used to embody the '**Arab identity**': for example, Khadra (1985) stresses the role of the prophetic/visionary leader, and Hawi (1982) provides a model of the Islamic leader with specific traits.
7. Jreisat (1990) found that a major distinction between the motivations of Arab and US managers was that the Arab managers had a very high sense of **public responsibility**, with a sense of nationhood (an extension of the tribe) being a strong source of fulfilment.
8. Muna (1980) interviewed 52 Arab executives, finding that most saw themselves as being head of a family, with their employees as family members.

Research Methods and Scope

We aim to do two things: firstly, to identify the components of the Gulf leadership style, as espoused by Gulf Arab leaders in positions of corporate authority. While this is not evidence of actual practice, it is a useful indicator of leadership beliefs. Secondly, we aim to consider the implications of this leadership style for HRM policies and practices.

We focus on GCC Arab nationals in both the public and the private sector. We encouraged the leaders themselves to express what they felt to be the components of their leadership style. We first captured a sample of these voices, then modelled the principal components being described, and finally tested for the consistency of description to identify a definable Gulf Arab leadership style.

When exploring dimensions that cannot be predicted or represented by closed multiple choice, ranking, or similar questions, then open-ended questions are recommended (Ballou 2008). The disadvantages of open-ended design include the effort required to extract useful valid data, potential bias from coders, and lower practical sample sizes. The choice, in this case, was whether to adopt a previously defined model of leadership characteristics in order to deploy a pre-defined instrument (for example, the GLOBE study as reported by House et al. 2002) or to allow the interviewees to express their views and experiences in an unstructured way (for example, Al Ismaily's (2004) study of Omani organizational culture). The advantage of the former is that it allows comparative analysis between stylistic clusters and is simple to analyze and therefore allows large samples. The advantage of the latter is that the analysis requires no pre-judgment of the answers and the data will be richer and more representative of the leaders' own beliefs.

Given that we sought to identify the components of the Gulf Arab leadership style from the interviewees' espoused views, rather than applying a pre-determined model, it was decided to invest the time and effort required for conducting semi-structured interviews, and thus to limit the number of responding interviewees to 50. We also sought to mitigate potential bias or inaccuracy by using two independent coders and inter-coder reliability testing to highlight potential weaknesses in the coding method, such as unclear categories or individual bias.

After experimenting with recording devices and written notes, it was decided to use written notes, as the recording method proved constraining for the interviewees. A test coding of one set of notes with a transcript of the same conversation found no material differences in the content noted. It was also decided, for consistency, to use one interviewer (one of the authors) to carry out the interviews and to use two different researchers to code the responses. We conducted semi-structured interviews with 50 senior Arab national leaders across the GCC, representing a mix of ages, countries, gender, and industrial sectors (see demographic below).

The interviews were conducted in 2011–2012. Each interview was scheduled to last up to one hour and included the following questions:

1. As you look ahead to the next 12–18 months, what do you see as being the five most critical opportunities or challenges for the GCC?
2. How would you describe the leadership style that you want for your organization?
3. Is there a distinctive Gulf Arab leadership style (0–5 where 0 = no, none)?
4. How would you describe the components of a distinct 'Gulf Arab leadership style'?
5. How would you describe the main determinants of a distinct 'Gulf Arab leadership style'?

The analysis in this paper utilizes the responses to Questions 3, 4, and 5. For Question 3, the scores between 0 and 5 were averaged and a standard deviation calculated. The scores were correlated with the demographic data (taking into account sample sizes) to explore, for example, whether female leaders' opinions varied from those of male leaders. For Question 4, to avoid pre-conceived categorization, the two coders were not provided with a coding framework of possible components but each independently derived a coding framework from their analysis of the responses. Two researchers (an Arab student and a UK consultant) independently coded each response. They then determined if a single definition could be assigned to each of their components. For the most frequently cited components there was a clear correspondence. Question 5 was analyzed using the same methodology.

Interviews with 50 Senior Corporate Leaders

Of the respondents, 84% were male and 22% were aged under 30, with 46% aged between 30 and 50, and 32% over 50. The respondents were nationals of various GCC countries and from a range of industrial sectors (see Figs 3.1 and 3.2).

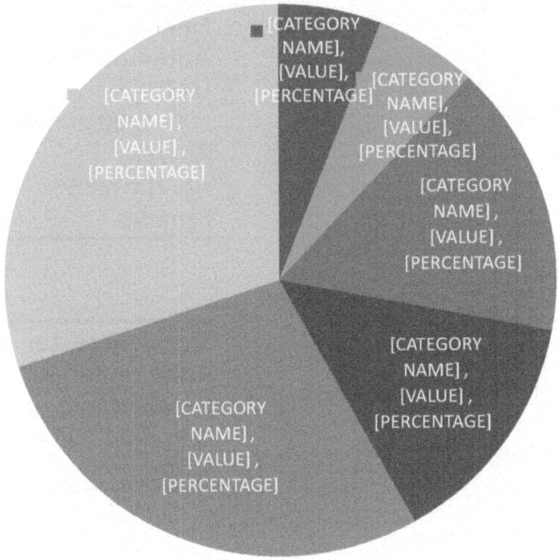

Fig. 3.1 Pie chart representing the nationality respondents

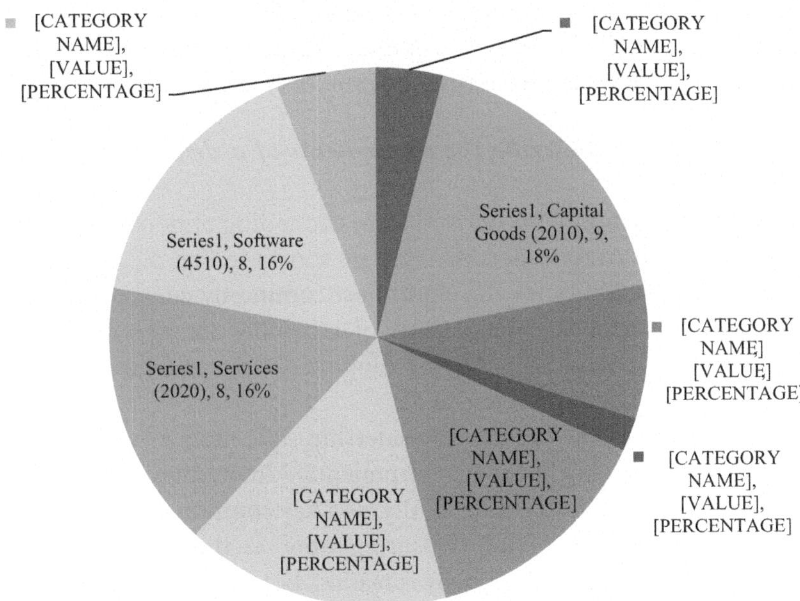

Fig. 3.2 Pie chart representing the range of industrial sectors of respondents

Table 3.1 Groups MOST likely to think there was a distinctive Gulf leadership style

Financial sector	5.00
Automobile sector	4.75
UAE	4.23
500–1000 employees	4.20
Kuwait	4.17
Aged over 50	4.15
Females	3.88

Table 3.2 Groups LEAST likely to think there was a distinctive Gulf leadership style

Software sector	2.64
Aged under 30	2.82
Oman	2.88
Less than 500 employees	3.08
Males	3.71

The mean score for the question 'Is there a distinctive Gulf Arab leadership style?' was 3.74 (where 0 = no distinctive Gulf Arab leadership style and 5 = extremely distinctive). Although there are too few responses in each demographic category to conduct formal significance testing, the results do suggest some interesting differences (Tables 3.1 and 3.2):

How would you describe the components of a distinct 'Gulf Arab leadership style'?

The ordered components derived from the coding of potential components of the Gulf Arab leadership style are shown in Fig. 3.3.

Inter-coder reliability for the eight most commonly cited components exceeded 90%, with the major tests of reliability (Scott's Pi, Cohen's Kappa, and Krippendorff's Alpha) ranging from moderately to very strongly reliable (Tables 3.3 and 3.4).

The attributes of the Gulf Arab leadership style most espoused by the respondents fall into eight broad components. Almost all the respondents espoused 'leading as head of the family' as a key component, with 'building lasting relationships' and 'treasuring time' as the next equal most commonly identified, followed by 'creating bold visions'. As with any such cultural or anthropological study, there are often more differences within any group than between groups, so the findings are summaries of

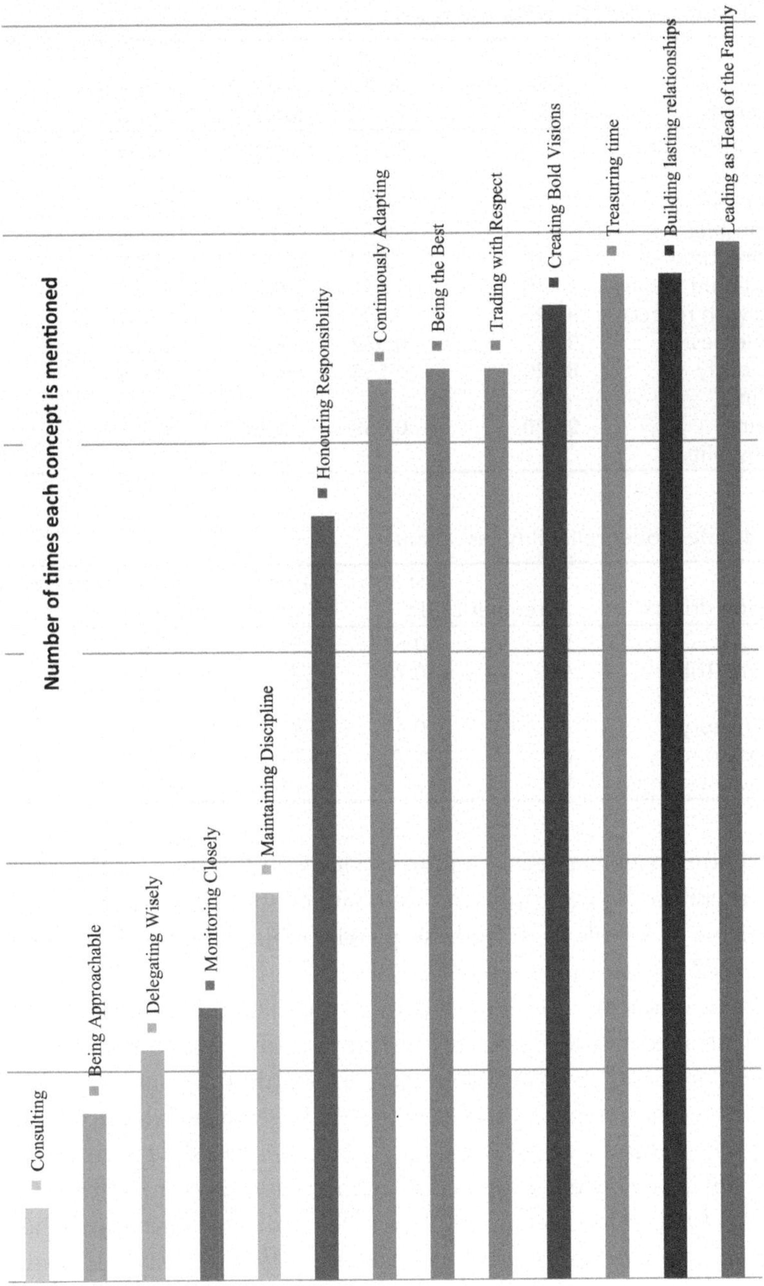

Fig. 3.3 Number of times each concept related to a distinct 'Gulf Arab leadership style' is mentioned

Table 3.3 Inter-coder reliability test results

Components	Percent agreement (%)	Scott's Pi	Cohen's Kappa	Krippendorff's Alpha
Leading as head of the family	98	0.657	0.658	0.66
Building lasting relationships	92.20	0.292	0.292	0.299
Treasuring time	92.20	0.292	0.292	0.299
Creating bold visions	94.10	0.634	0.635	0.638
Trading with respect	90.20	0.609	0.612	0.613
Being the best	98	0.922	0.922	0.923
Continuously adapting	88.20	0.555	0.56	0.56
Honouring responsibility	90.20	0.759	0.76	0.761

Table 3.4 Inter-coder reliability test results 2

Underlying drivers	% agreement	Scott's Pi	Cohen's Kappa	Krippendorff's Alpha
Islam	90	0.56	0.56	0.56
Traditional/Tribal culture	90	0.76	0.76	0.76
Trading history	78	0.41	0.41	0.42
Innate personality	88	0.70	0.71	0.71
Family business model	92	0.73	0.73	0.73

a modal consensus between a range of views and opinions. The results should therefore be interpreted as illustrative—but they do suggest the components of a Gulf Arab leadership style, which might inform a contingent HRM system for the GCC.

The value of the methodology is demonstrated, as the component most often mentioned, 'Leading as Head of the Family', would probably not have been provided as an available category within previously developed leadership instruments. On the other hand, it is not possible to directly compare the components of the Gulf Arab leadership style with components of any other style. Compared to an international comparative study such as GLOBE (House et al. 2002), which uses a standard multi-choice instrument, we can say that the respondents *believe* the style is distinctive, but we cannot directly demonstrate that it *is*, compared to, say, a Japanese leadership style, as the constructs used to describe each style are not equivalent. On the other hand, the literature on leadership styles does suggest that the major components of the Gulf Arab leadership style identified here are different to the top characteristics of, for example, US leaders, typically characterized as assertive, performance-orientated, and highly individualistic (Sanchez-Runde et al. 2011).

The top four components are now elaborated and discussed below.

1. *Leading as Head of the Family*: This component was noted by all respondents, with nearly 98% agreement and with inter-coder reliability of 0.66. The Gulf Arab leader sees the company or their team as like their family—with familial obligations and responsibilities for the leaders and the led. Many of the respondents stated that 'Loyalty is more important than effectiveness'. Subordinates will often quote older team members—'we must learn from our fathers'—and tend to show respect for experience, age, and knowledge. Every employee is made to feel part of the 'family', with corresponding obligations and benefits. This is particularly interesting where, as in most large GCC organizations, there is a mix of expatriates, with different natural leadership or organizational styles. Some less functional aspects mentioned by respondents were that bad news is very often hidden and disagreement with or challenge to the ideas of leaders is extremely rare. Poor performance is not resolved, provided loyalty is demonstrated, and efficiency can be a very low priority.
2. *Building Relationships*: This component was noted at 92% agreement but with a more moderate inter-coder reliability of 0.3. For the Gulf Arab leader, relationships are extremely important in all aspects of life, including business, and the power of relationships sets them apart. So the leader actively seeks to build wide and influential relationships, and operates in a manner that builds trust in others.
3. *Treasuring Time*: This component was noted at 92% agreement but with a more moderate inter-coder reliability of 0.3. The Gulf Arab leader sees time as a precious resource to be utilized and enjoyed where, as one respondent put it, 'priorities drive our time and schedule, our schedule does not drive our priorities'.

4. *Creating Bold Visions*: This component was noted at 94% agreement with reliability of ~0.6. Our interviewees stressed that a Gulf Arab leader seeks out and embraces challenge—'always taking the tough road if it is the right one'. The leader, we were told, sees the 'impossible' as an enjoyable goal (like a mountain to climb or a race to run) and creates and communicates a highly stretching and bold vision for the future. Understanding and 'buy-in' to a long-term vision is seen as being far more important for success than adherence to short-term plans or efficiency (Fig. 3.4).

How would you describe the main determinants of a distinct Gulf Arab leadership style?

The most cited underlying determinant is **Islam**, with a percentage agreement of 90% and inter-coder reliability of 0.56. **Traditional/tribal culture** scored 90% agreement with 0.76 inter-coder reliability. **Trading history** was mentioned by many, but with less agreement between the coders at 78%, with inter-coder reliability of 0.41. **Innate personality** scored 88%

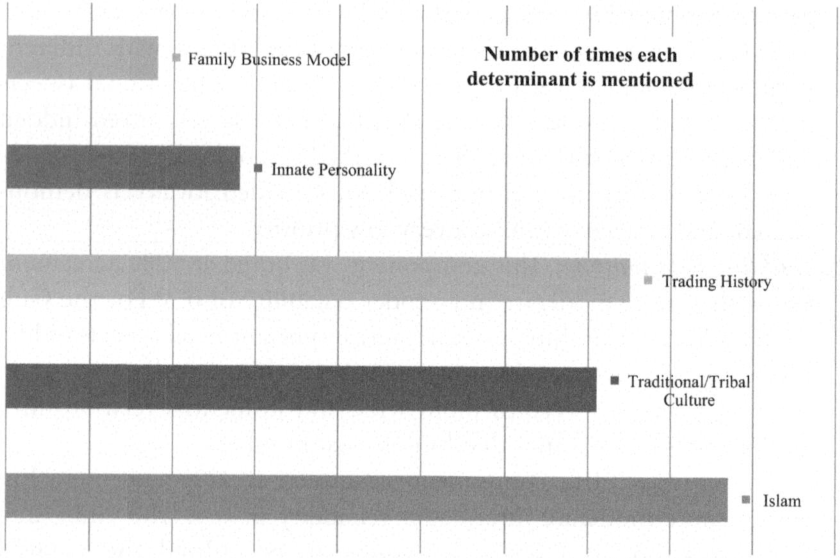

Fig. 3.4 Number of times each determinant of *a distinct 'Gulf Arab leadership style'* is mentioned

with inter-coder reliability of 0.70. **Family business model** was noted by about 12% but with inter-coder agreement of 92% and reliability of 0.73.

Implications for HRM

Efforts are under way, for example through the Arabian Society for Human Resource Management (ASHRM), to introduce appropriate training and certification for GCC human resources (HR) professionals. We consider how the Gulf Arab leadership style might influence a GCC contingent HRM, using four areas noted by the Chartered Institute of Personnel and Development (CIPD) in their HR Profession Map (http://www.cipd.co.uk/cipd-hr-profession/hr-profession-map/):

1. *Resourcing and Talent Planning*: The Gulf Arab leadership style might suggest a weighting to loyalty as a recruitment criterion and, in consequence, a disposition to recruit members of the extended family or people who come with strong recommendation. It was noted in several of the interviews that leaders would apply different criteria depending on whether a role was 'part of the business group' (loyalty being uppermost) or outside the core (capability being uppermost). Much has been written on the concept of '*wasta*' (or 'use of influence') in Arab business practices and, for example, its influence in talent resourcing and development (for a review see Smith et al. 2012).
2. *Learning and Talent Development*: Respondents suggested that, in a patriarchal hierarchy, much applied learning most effectively takes place by watching and listening to 'father figures' or superiors, with more weight given to the words and actions of the most superior. As well as developing skill, this serves the purpose of reinforcing and confirming respect upwards and nurturing downwards, and preserving the leader's authority and influence over approaches to work and culture within the organization.
3. *Performance and Reward*: The preference for a person-oriented style means that the executives interviewed here value loyalty, and similarly Muna (1980) found that around 70% of Arab executives valued loyalty more highly than efficiency.

4. *Employee Relations and Engagement*: Interviewees suggested that given the obligations of the leader to look after the employees and the existence of mechanisms such as the *majlis* (a regular open forum where anyone can raise grievances or issues with the leader), there was no need for collective representation.

Conclusion

This chapter has identified the key components of an espoused Gulf Arab leadership style and suggested ways in which this might affect the practice of HRM in the countries of the GCC. This explores a relatively neglected area. Further research might explore the reality in practice of this espoused style and its actual impact on the operation of effective HRM policies and practices in the GCC, including through large-sample studies of HR practices and their 'universal' or 'GCC contingent' nature.

Analyzing the 50 interviews we conducted suggests that there is a distinct Gulf Arab leadership style being espoused which, within its context, may be highly functional and indeed may provide a differentiating capability and source of competitive advantage. This leadership style, along with other factors such as local regulatory frameworks and religious perspective, suggests that a contingent model of HRM is appropriate for the GCC—which may utilize global best practice where appropriate, but needs also to be cognizant of the distinctive circumstances of the GCC. Certainly, the influence of the West is increased as organizations within the GCC employ and work with large numbers of expatriate staff, and also through owning and managing overseas subsidiaries in non-Arab countries. An informed, considered, and flexible application of a blend of the best management practices from other cultures, combined with the most valuable elements of the Gulf Arab leadership style, is therefore called for. This has implications for the professionalism and codification of HRM in the region, which cannot adequately be predicated on any of the current, predominantly Western, HRM standards or certifications. Here, too, a contingent approach may prove to be the more appropriate.

Bibliography

Adair, J. (2010). *The leadership of Muhammad*. London: Kogan Page Publishers.

Al Abed, I., & Hellyer, P. (2001). *United Arab Emirates: A new perspective*. London: Trident Press.

Al Ismaily, S. N. (2004). Leadership dynamics in Oman. *Oman Economic Review, 11*(52), 21–43.

Al Omian, M., & Weir, D. (2005). *Leadership in the Arab world*. Amman, Jordan: University of Jordan.

Ali, A. J. (1990). Management theory in a transitional society: The Arab's experience. *International Studies of Management & Organization, 20*(3), 7–35.

Ali, A. J., & Camp, R. C. (1995). Teaching management in the Arab world: Confronting illusions. *International Journal of Educational Management, 9*(2), 10–17.

Allen, K. E., Bordas, J., Hickman, G. R., Matusak, L. R., Sorenson, G. J., & Whitmire, K. J. (2006). Leadership in the twenty-first century. *IEEE Engineering Management Review, 34*(2), 60–67.

Aycan, Z., Al-Hamadi, A. B., Davis, A., & Budhwar, P. (2007). Cultural orientations and preferences for HRM policies and practices: The case of Oman. *The International Journal of Human Resource Management, 18*(1), 11–32.

Ayubi, N. (1988). Arab bureaucrats: Overstaffing and multiplicity of functions. *Arab Future, 108*, 85–99.

Ballou, J. (2008). Open-ended question. *Encyclopedia of Survey Research Methods, 43*, 548–550.

Bass, B. M. (1985). *Leadership and performance beyond expectations*. New York/London: Free Press/Collier Macmillan.

Beekun, R. I., & Badawi, J. A. (1999). *Leadership: An Islamic perspective*. Beltsville, MD: Amana.

Budhwar, P., & Mallahi, K. (2006). *Managing human resources in the Middle East*. London: Routledge.

Cummins, J. I. (2012). Hearts and minds: US foreign policy and anti-Americanism in the Middle East an analysis of public perceptions from 2002–2011. Doctoral dissertation, Wright State University.

Day, D. V., & Lord, R. G. (1988). Executive leadership and organizational performance: Suggestions for a new theory and methodology. *Journal of Management, 14*(3), 453–464.

Fox, J. W., Mourtada-Sabbah, N., & al-Mutawa, M. (2006). The Arab Gulf region: Traditionalism globalized or globalization traditionalized? In J. W. Fox,

N. Mourtada-Sabbah, & M. al-Mutawa (Eds.), *Globalization and the Gulf* (pp. 3–59). London: Routledge.

Fromherz, A. J. (2012). *Qatar: A modern history*. Washington, DC: Georgetown University Press.

Hawi, S. (1982). *Fisoul Fi alamrh wa alamer. Lectures on leadership and leader*. Annan, Jordan: Al-Sharg Printing Co.

Hofstede, G., & Peterson, M. F. (2000). Culture: National values and organizational practices. *Handbook of Organizational Culture and Climate*, 401–416.

Hofstede, G. H., & Hofstede, G. (2001). *Culture's consequences: Comparing values, behaviors, institutions and organizations across nations*. Thousand Oaks, CA: Sage.

House, R., Javidan, M., Hanges, P., & Dorfman, P. (2002). Understanding cultures and implicit leadership theories across the globe: An introduction to project GLOBE. *Journal of World Business, 37*(1), 3–10.

Jreisat, J. E. (1990). Administrative change and the Arab manager. *Public Administration and Development, 10*(4), 413–421.

Kabasakal, H., & Bodur, M. (2002). Arabic cluster: A bridge between East and West. *Journal of World Business, 37*(1), 40–54.

Khadra, B. (1985). Leadership, ideology and development in the Middle East. *The Middle East*, 109–119.

Lacey, R. (2009). *Inside the kingdom*. London: Random House.

Maslow, A. H. (1943). A theory of human motivation. *Psychological Review, 50*(4), 370–396.

Muna, F. A. (1980). *The Arab executive*. New York: St. Martin's Press.

Muna, F. A. (2003). *Seven metaphors on management: Tools for managers in the Arab world*. Aldershot, UK: Gower Publishing Company.

Nusair, N. (1983). Human nature and motivation in Islam. *Islamic Quarterly, 29*(3), 148–164.

Sanchez-Runde, C., Nardon, L., & Steers, R. M. (2011). Looking beyond Western leadership models: Implications for global managers. *Organizational Dynamics, 40*(3), 207–213.

Shi, X., & Wang, J. (2011). Interpreting hofstede model and globe model: Which way to go for cross-cultural research? *International Journal of Business and Management, 6*(5), 93.

Smith, W. K., Besharov, M. L., Wessels, A. K., & Chertok, M. (2012). A paradoxical leadership model for social entrepreneurs: Challenges, leadership skills, and pedagogical tools for managing social and commercial demands. *Academy of Management Learning & Education, 11*(3), 463–478.

Trompenaars, F., & Hampden-Turner. C. (1998). *Riding the waves of culture: Understanding cultural diversity in business.*

Trompenaars, F., & Woolliams, P. (2003). *Business across cultures.* Chichester, UK: Capstone.

Whiteoak, J. W., Crawford, N. G., & Mapstone, R. H. (2006). Impact of gender and generational differences in work values and attitudes in an Arab culture. *Thunderbird International Business Review, 48*(1), 77–91.

Yasin, M. M., & Stahl, M. J. (1990). An investigation of managerial motivational effectiveness in the Arab culture. *International Studies of Management & Organization, 20*(3), 69–78.

Yousef, D. A. (2001). Islamic work ethic-A moderator between organizational commitment and job satisfaction in a cross-cultural context. *Personnel Review, 30*(2), 152–169.

4

Development of Education and Its Impact on Middle Eastern Societies

George M. Jabbour, Linda A. Livingstone, and Lindos Daou

Introduction

Education is considered a basic foundation of economic and social development in all countries. The existence of educated people in society is essential to drive business development contributing to economic prosperity and a better social environment. Nowadays, with growing competition in the educational sector worldwide and in the Middle East in particular, educational institutions are recognizing their role in shaping society and the leaders of future generations. Thus, more emphasis is being put on education and its development so that institutions can stay up to date with recent developments in the areas of technological advances, pedagogical tools, and research methods in order to reach this goal.

G.M. Jabbour • L.A. Livingstone
The George Washington University School of Business, George Washington University, Washington, DC, USA

L. Daou (✉)
USEK School of Business, Holy Spirit Univerity of Kaslik, Jounieh, Lebanon

N. Azoury (ed.), *Business and Society in the Middle East*,
DOI 10.1007/978-3-319-48857-8_4

Quality education does not, however, guarantee sustainable economic development. In a poor economic system we observe high unemployment rates instead of better living standards and higher salaries (World Bank 1999), even if the country has a strong educational system. Hence, education should go hand in hand with broader economic initiatives to best address society's needs and to drive economic prosperity. Therefore, we consider educational institutions as entities integral to society since they have a significant influence on the development and progress of people's lives and thus society more broadly. Educated people, such as architects, physicians, and lawmakers will be the backbone of society. If citizens are educated and well prepared, they will be instrumental in developing a modern society; otherwise, they will be influential in writing a story of limited development and demise.

Overview of Education in the Middle East

Middle Eastern countries have many characteristics in common including, but not limited to, language and religion. They speak Arabic and they follow, in the vast majority of cases, Islam. These countries are facing increasing challenges because of the expansion of basic education in the region. Their institutions have significant differences in linguistic and cultural terms, and these have a large impact on education and diversity. Despite these differences, institutions manage to coexist even inside national borders. They are often driven by a centralized command and control management culture that limits classroom initiatives which foster creativity and learning. Most importantly, the value of education is not uniform; in some countries learning is perceived as very important, while in others it is considered an unwarranted opportunity cost because of the pressing economic conditions that oblige children to drop out of school to start working early (World Bank 1999).

Education systems in the Middle East are heavily bureaucratic, and recruitment of faculty and students is often based on connections rather than qualifications. Nepotism is common practice in recruitment for administrative positions as well. Most institutions in the region are public, except for those in Lebanon, Jordan, and Palestine. Planning is disorganized and incoherent, and funds are seldom allocated for poor rural areas because urban areas and other locations where wealthy groups reside receive priority.

In the Middle East, education has traditionally been considered a privilege for wealthy families. But many donor agencies and promoters have emphasized the importance of early education and considered investment in it as more important than funding higher education, in order to break the intergenerational poverty cycle (Young and Mundial 1996). This investment will have a social impact and is a starting point for the development of societies through the enhancement of social status among a wider range of people, and creating opportunities for the educated to work in better positions with higher salaries. This presents an opportunity for learners who are eager to shift their social class through education, which enhances social mobility. Accordingly, Arab governments have adopted social and educational policies to support and increase early childhood programs and initiatives. As a result, net enrollment in primary education rose from 86% to 94% between 2000 and 2010 (World Bank 2014a). Some countries such as Jordan and Egypt have tried to integrate early childhood programs in their educational planning system; and Iran provided financial support for early education programs through the Ministry of Education's public institutions (Sabbaghian 1992). It should be noted that the education sector in the Middle East would not have continued without the financial and moral support of international actors in the field of Early Childhood Care and Education, including UNICEF (United Nations International Children Emergency Fund), UNESCO (United Nations Educational, Scientific and Cultural Organization), Save the Children, the Bernard van Leer Foundation, the High/Scope Foundation, and the World Bank. In this context, Figure 4.1 shows youth literacy rates for those aged between 15 and 24 in the region. We observe in general an increasing trend in literacy in Middle Eastern countries, especially during 2013–2015. Nevertheless we can clearly see that literacy in Iraq follows a strictly declining curve, but conversely literacy in Syria shows an upward trend after 2004. This is because of the huge migration of Syrian refugees to neighboring countries, where they are continuing their primary and secondary education (Fig. 4.1).

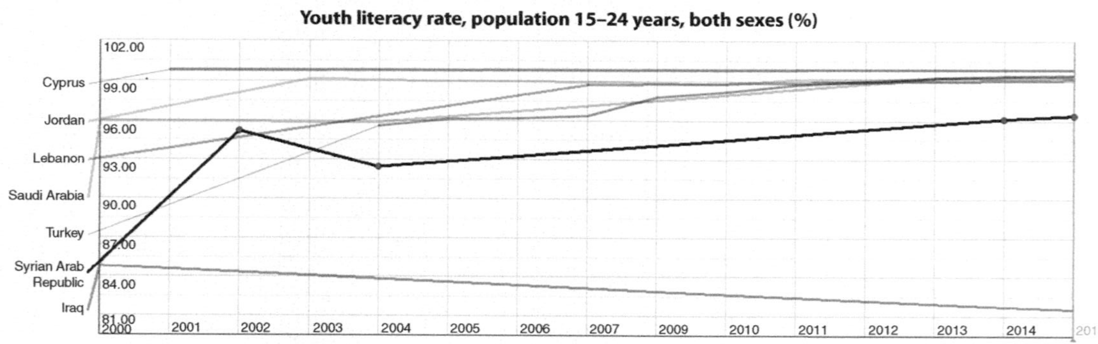

Fig. 4.1 Trends for literacy for youth rates. Source: UNESCO Institute for Statistics, National literacy rates for youths (15–24) and adults (15+), available from UIS website, http://www.uis.unesco.org

Despite all those efforts, women, rural populations, and the poor in general have not been served well in different countries in the region. Existing models and systems do not meet human resources needs for the region, and they have failed to have a significant impact on social development despite expenditure on education, which is among the highest in the developing regions (Christina et al. 2007). In other words, education is not meeting the needs of society. For instance, as Fig. 4.2 shows, we can observe an increasing trend in unemployment rates in the Middle Eastern countries. Iraq and the Syrian Arab Republic have significantly higher unemployment levels than other countries owing to the unstable political situation and war. Yet we think that a primary reason for high unemployment in the region is the lack of student orientation, advice, and guidance that helps students to choose their areas of specialization. These high unemployment rates are mainly noticeable in several saturated fields. For instance, there are 3.54 physicians per 1000 people according to the CIA World Fact Book (2009), but there is a significant deficit in qualified employees in many specializations and majors. There is little interest in vocational education but strong demand for fields leading to white collar jobs, which help people achieve higher social status and prestige.

Challenges

Education in the Middle East has many challenges, in part because the region is constantly struggling to keep up with international educational standards. One challenge is based on the region's success in improving elementary through high school education over the last decades. The significant increase in the number of high school graduates created a serious demand for higher education which institutions at that level are unable to absorb and accommodate.

Other challenges in the region include high student–faculty ratios, low salaries, lack of academic freedom, poor infrastructure, and poor research facilities. This is considered a strong incentive for governments to establish high professional standards (Massialas 1991). In addition, overcrowding in several Middle Eastern countries led to inadequate classrooms, laboratories, libraries, and technological facilities. Moreover, teaching is

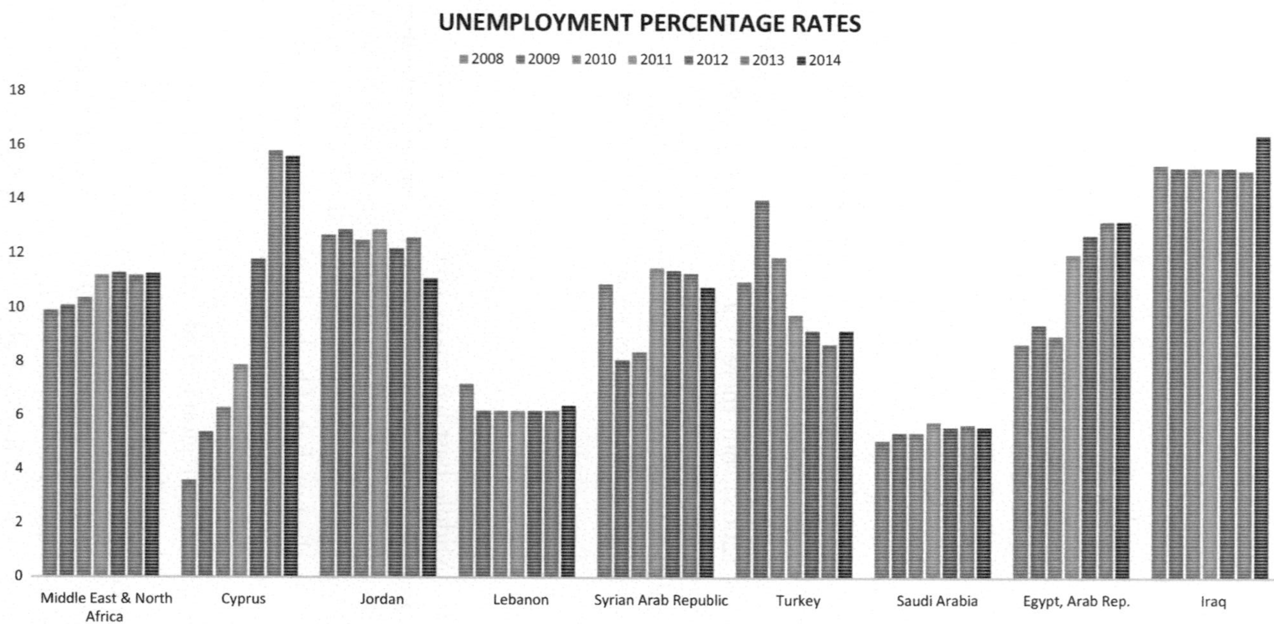

Fig. 4.2 Unemployment rates by country. Source: International Labour Organization, Key Indicators of the Labour Market database (2016)

lecture-centered with minimal use of experiential and practical learning pedagogies. Governance is usually centralized, with inadequate participation of faculty and senior staff from different units. Opportunities to access secondary and higher education require that students pass national or regional examinations at the end of primary and/or secondary cycles, except for Jordan where admission to advanced cycles is not based on performance in the primary stage. This prevents a large number of interested people from attending higher education institutions in the region. For instance, in Iran only 10% of the applicants are admitted to colleges (World Bank 1999). In other nations, such as Lebanon and Jordan, higher education is considered a highly valued privilege; students tend to work hard to earn the best grades they can so they can successfully compete to secure their spots at institutions of higher education (Ellington 2005). With the rise of globalization and the digital world, primary education has received greater attention because parents want their children to receive it; and governments are investing in public schools to provide quality primary education. In Figure 4.3, we notice that educational attainment of the population aged 25 years and older has been, in general, an increasing trend in various countries of the MENA (Middle East and North Africa) region (Fig. 4.3).

International and civil conflicts have been a constant and major cause of recession in education in terms of human and physical capital. People are temporarily or permanently displaced; physical and social infrastructure has been destroyed. During the war in Lebanon, teachers had great difficulty in crossing zones of control to reach their schools. In Yemen, schools were destroyed in 1994 during the civil war. The situation is no better now, with renewed conflicts and fighting across the region. Educational facilities were destroyed or severely damaged during the Iran–Iraq war and Gulf wars, and rebuilding educational infrastructure was not a priority for rehabilitation projects in post-conflict situations (World Bank 1999). Finally, with the recent crisis in Syria, many students have been displaced and educational authorities have had to deal with the ever-growing wave of school-age refugees especially in Jordan and Lebanon. According to UN projections, even if the crisis were to end immediately, it could take almost ten years for the displaced refugees to return to Syria. Of course, immediate action is needed to respond to

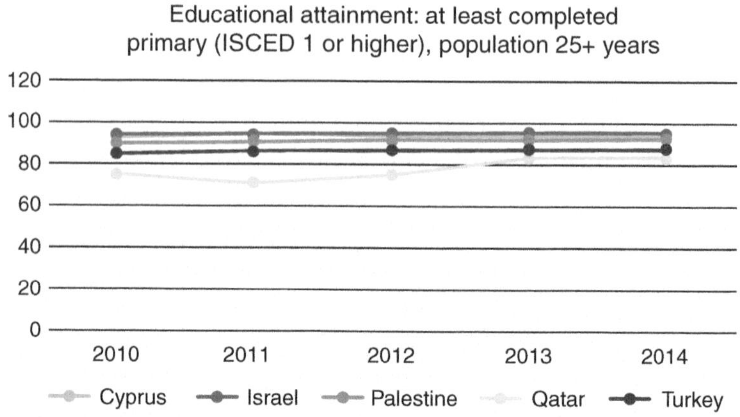

Fig. 4.3 Educational attainment of the population aged 25 years and older. Source: UNESCO Institute for Statistics (2016)

the humanitarian crisis, but the next step is to deal with the growth and development of school-age refugees currently in neighboring countries (World Bank 2014a), to ensure their education is not stifled while they are displaced.

Current Trends in Higher Education (Opportunities)

Higher education in the Middle East has great potential to develop and grow owing to the boost in population and the need for educated people to run emerging and growing businesses in the region. The main paradox, however, remains in the dramatic growth in demand for education and the reduced quality of teaching and scholarship. Higher education has expanded from eight universities in the region in 1940 to several hundred institutions offering post-secondary education today. Although this growth rate is considerable, the Middle East is still far behind developed countries. In addition, this impressive expansion in higher education facilities has not been able to meet the demand in some countries owing to the exceptional demographic change. An estimate of the MENA population in 1980 was 168 million, while it had increased to around 396 million in 2015 (World Bank, World Development Indicators 2016). This has significantly affected the number of educational institutions in the region, and many of them are striving to provide quality education through both national and international accreditations.

One of the rising trends in higher education in the region is the increase in institutionalization and privatization. Lebanon is the only Arab country where the majority of higher education is private; but Palestine and Jordan are moving toward that model as well. Qatar and the United Arab Emirates have also begun to experiment with privatization in higher education (Heyneman 2002). As privatized Western brand institutions increase in number, one strategy is to import foreign curricula, aiming at the replication of quality programs in a timely and effective way. Despite the strong interest in education, public financial support is still on average a small percentage of gross domestic product (GDP) in Middle Eastern countries, as noted in Fig. 4.4. But the numbers in some countries are comparable to those in UK, Canada, and the USA (World Bank 2013).

Another trend in the Arab world is strong governmental intervention in the appointment of heads of universities, based on nepotism, personal interest, and influence, rather than academic and professional qualifications. Such trends may not be in the best interest of educational institutions' autonomy and development. Modern Arab universities tend to be bureaucratic and centralized, strictly adhering to civil service rules and policies instead of striving towards academic freedom and autonomy. Consequently there is minimal statutory basis for faculty participation in the decision-making process (Massialas and Jarrar 1991).

Currently, students are determined to choose the university that provides them with the most solid and rigorous education, which will in turn help them to have attractive work opportunities. This issue has led university administrators in Sultanate Oman to design master's specializations according to vacancies available in large companies and the governmental sector. This strategy perfectly serves students' ultimate objective of enrolling in a university which can land them a job. On another level, the university is reaching its goal by serving the needs of society and shaping qualified persons to occupy highly ranked positions. Yet education in the Middle East is more often influenced by cultural trends and prestige, especially for those who obtain their degrees from

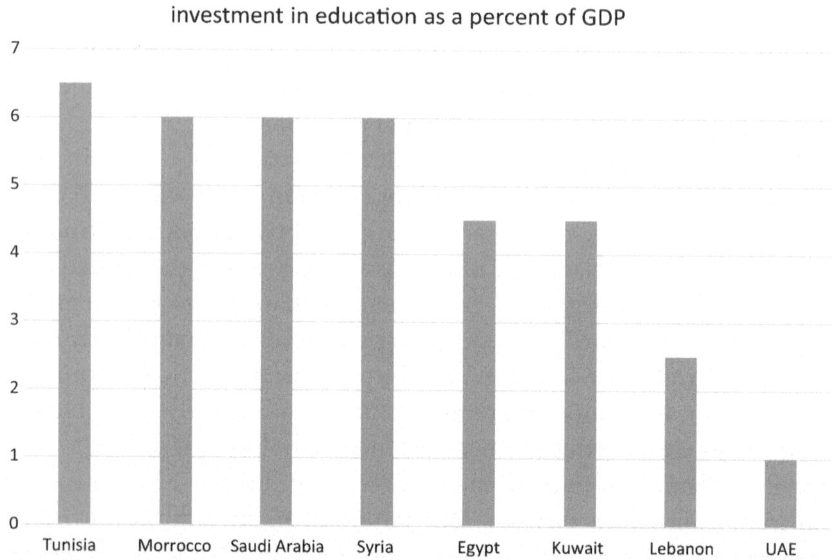

Fig. 4.4 Public investment in education in MENA countries (percentage of GDP). Source: World Bank 2013

European or American universities. The local perception is that Western education represents added value and prestige, and provides its recipients with a head start over other candidates.

Role of Women in the Education Cycle

Middle Eastern countries have different levels of political development, economic affluence, and educational achievement, and these differences contribute to a distinctive role and status of women in each country. Lebanese and Egyptian women enjoy a long history of educational provision, while it is still a recent phenomenon for Kuwaiti, Saudi Arabian, and Omani women. In these countries, women's access to schools was limited, but now, they are allowed to attend some educational institutions, and some affluent families can even afford to have private tutors at home.

Recently, a larger number of women have been completing their compulsory education, thus leading to improvements in health and nutrition status for them and their children, and raising their stature in society. The increasing literacy rate allows the educated workforce to quickly learn and adapt to new technologies and processes, and will increase the number of people interested in pursuing secondary and tertiary education. A report published by the World Bank Group shows that women with little or no education at all have a high chance of being married at a very early age, suffering domestic violence, living in poverty, and having limited access to and control over household and health spending, all of which has a negative impact on their children and communities. (World Bank 2014b). We can see from Table 4.1 that the percentage of illiterate women is relatively low except for Syria, Iraq, Egypt and Saudi Arabia owing to a range of different reasons, mainly cultural, social, political, and economic. We may also note that the percentage of illiteracy among the younger generation of females is decreasing. In other words, fewer females aged between 15 and 24 are illiterate than those over the age of 15 (Table 4.1).

A significant number of girls who are making the transition to higher education choose traditionally female fields of study. It is not because they are uninterested in male-oriented specialization, nor because of their qualifications, but simply because the social norms and culture of the region limit their choices. In secondary education, gender disparity is evident in the fields of study chosen by the students. For instance, the fields of humanities, medicine, and education are traditionally deemed appropriate for women since they lead to respectable, sex-segregated employment. Historically, STEM (Science, Technology, Engineering and Mathematics) academic fields were not available for women, who had access only to education development and humanities. This resulted in a surplus of humanities graduates and a serious shortage of graduates coming from technical and vocational education. Therefore, there existed a mismatch between university graduates and the needs of the labor market. Nevertheless, when girls were allowed access to "male-dominated" fields such as agriculture and engineering, they had an equal success rate to boys, and sometimes higher. Girls in Kuwait achieved higher scores than boys in secondary examinations and in science subjects (Al-Methun and Wilkenson 1988).

Today, more Middle Eastern women have moved to the formal labor market and into positions of importance in political and social circles,

Table 4.1 Trends for illiteracy for females

	Percentage of population over age 15 who are illiterate, 2000	Number of people over age 15 who are illiterate (thousands), 2000	Percentage of population ages 15–24 who are illiterate, 2000	Number of people ages 15–24 who are illiterate (thousands), 2000
	Female	Female	Female	Female
Middle East and North Africa	42	50,057	23	8585
Egypt	56	12,253	37	2500
Iraq	77	5070	71	1593
Jordan	16	220	1	3
Kuwait	20	103	7	15
Lebanon	20	246	7	23
Qatar	17	21	3	1
Saudi Arabia	33	1723	10	187
Syria	40	1879	21	376
Turkey	24	5453	6	392
United Arab Emirates	21	117	6	10
Average	32.4	2708.5	16.9	510

Source: UNESCO Institute for Statistics, "Literacy Statistics" (www.uis.unesco.org, accessed March 11, 2003); United Nations Development Programme, Human Development Report 2002; UN Statistics Division, The World's Women 2000: Trends and Statistics

and the role of women as "housewife/lactating mother" has been deeply changed. The family structure has been altered from extended family model to smaller family units. Nuclear families are increasing, particularly in urban areas. Ultimately, alterations in family structures and socio-economic levels in the region have had a direct impact on values, attitudes, and child-rearing habits, leading families to look for childcare alternatives (UNESCO 1995). Nowadays, women's education is an effective investment in developing countries, regardless of whether they work or stay at home. Women will have a positive influence in their families, in areas that include better health and nutrition, improved child spacing, lower infant mortality, and enhanced educational attainment for their children (Dervis 1998). Figure 4.5 shows the trend of higher life expectancy rates

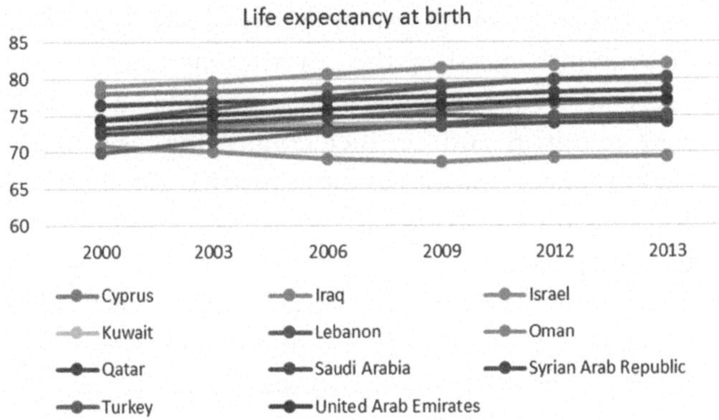

Fig. 4.5 Life expectancy at birth. Source: UNESCO Institute of Statistics (2016)

in various countries of the Middle East, especially in Lebanon, which is mainly owing to qualified physicians and high-quality medical support and hospitals. On the other hand, the continued unrest in Iraq has led to a weak infrastructure and a deficit in qualified and skilled medical staff. As for other Middle Eastern countries, we can observe an increasing trend in higher life expectancy owing to advances in the medical sector and in pharmaceuticals, with more people attending medical schools.

As compared to the rest of the world, women's involvement in education in the Middle East is very encouraging. The average increase in female enrollment between 1990 and 2001 was 7%, as compared to 3% in the majority of developing countries (UNESCO 2003). Despite the significant quantitative expansion and development in recent years and closing of the gender gap in primary education, there is still significant room for improvement in female education in the region.

Educational Development Strategies

In order to secure a sustainable future for the region, a careful and well-structured strategic plan must be prepared to cope with and overcome the hurdles and ongoing changes. Hence, MENA countries have started to implement several strategies to improve the quality of their educational system. The strategies available are divided into five main areas:

- Simplifying the management system: Many of MENA's education systems are heavily influenced by the government and specifically managed by several ministries. This creates problems regarding the allocation of resources and conflict concerning new approaches to enhance performance. Consolidating ministries responsible for education and focusing on standards and quality will result in better performance and management.
- Decentralization: Increasing school autonomy over allocation of resources, pedagogical methods of instruction used, language of instruction, and course scheduling can improve the system over time. This creates better assessment of the needs and resources that will work best in each institution, resulting in improved efficiency and effectiveness of classroom activities and student learning.
- Aligning curriculum, teacher training, instruction, and assessment: These four key educational elements should be brought into line for the effective functioning of the system as a whole rather than as a series of unrelated stages. When those key elements are standardized and aligned, they will contribute to better results and more effective goal accomplishment. In addition, teachers need to develop strategies that include different learning styles among students.
- Professionalizing the teaching framework: This strategy can be accomplished through training before recruiting staff and in-service training on pedagogical aspects and on new innovations in the world of learning and education. Other important steps might include increasing incentives and salaries for teachers, recruiting from reliable and trusted sources, upgrading the qualification criteria, and increasing the number of PhD holders and experienced teaching staff.
- "Leapfrogging" through the use of technology: It is impossible to continue and progress in the higher education sector without integrating technology through various teaching methods. Research has demonstrated that students using traditional computer-based systems outperformed their colleagues who were taught without the use of such systems.

Throughout the past three decades, governments' primary concern in the Middle East has been to support educational institutions. This has contributed to an uncontrolled and unsustainable growth rate of enrollments and, unfortunately, declining quality. This has resulted in increased public debt, and therefore it has not been able to support public education to as great an extent as in the past. Consequently, the World Bank has intervened to recommend and encourage the establishment of private education institutions to help solve the problem (Schwartzman 1992). Therefore, a new role for the state has emerged, to monitor higher education institutions across public and private sectors to ensure that equity and quality are attained.

Conclusion

In a global world dominated by information and knowledge, education has become more significant in the development of society and the growth of global prosperity. Policymakers should continue to support education from different perspectives, providing sustainable funding, developing a standardized framework for education on different levels, and applying continuous assessment and reform to cope with evolving technological and pedagogical advancements. Furthermore, ongoing concerns need to be addressed. For example, how will education affect future generations? How can we best assess the costs and benefits of such policies? And what fields are needed to create more opportunities for fresh graduates (World Bank 1999).

Throughout this chapter, we have emphasized that educated individuals play a very important role in society; they occupy high-level and intellectual jobs, drive business development, and earn more, which leads to greater dignity of life and enhanced community development, as well as higher contributions to the tax base, which supports infrastructural and other public needs. Furthermore, education should lead to longer life expectancy and improved social status and access to networks. Education will also increase awareness, tolerance, and understanding of other people's culture, traditions, and behaviors, which should eventually lead to reduced violence and lower crime rates. As a result, democracy and social systems may develop to increase the quality of relationships between people and to improve living standards.

Education and society are two entities that are closely interwoven, with the output of a society's economic system closely affected by educational institutions' input and influence on the development of human capital. The role of education is to help build a better future for the coming generations and to equip society with world-class leaders who have vision, values, and intellect. The ultimate result is to move humankind further and further along a path toward innovation, advancement, and global prosperity.

Bibliography

Al-Methun, A. E., & Wilkenson, W. J. (1988). In support of a sociological explanation of sex differences in science and mathematics achievement: Evidence from Kuwaiti study of secondary school certificate examinations. *Research in Science and Technological Education, 6*(1), 91–101.

Christina, R., Mehran, G., & Mir, S. (2007). Education in the Middle East: Opportunities and challenges. In R. F. Arnove & C. A. Torres (Eds.), *Comparative education: The dialect of the global and local* (pp. 311–332). Lanham, MD: Rowman and Littlefield Publishers, Inc.

CIA/Central Intelligence Agency. (2009). The World Factbook. Lebanon. Retrieved September 8, 2013, from https://www.cia.gov/library/publications/the-world-factbook/fields/2226.html#le

Dervis, K. (1998). *Education in the Middle East & North Africa: A strategy towards learning for development.* Human Development Network.

Ellington, L. (2005). *Japanese education.* Japan Education. Retrieved January 22, 2006, from http://www.indiana.edu/~japan/digest5.html

Heyneman, S. (2002). Quality of Education. In W. A. Rugh (Ed.), Arab education: Tradition, growth and reform. *Middle East Journal, 56*(3), 410–411.

International Labour Organization, Key Indicators of the Labour Market Database. (2016). 9th ed. Retrieved from http://www.ilo.org/wcmsp5/groups/public/---dgreports/---stat/.../wcms_498929.pdf

Massialas, B. (1991). The Arab world. In P. G. Altbach (Ed.), *International higher education.* London: Garland.

Massialas, B., & Jarrar, S. A. (1991). *Education in the Arab world.* New York: Garland.

Sabbaghian, Z. (1992). Kindergarten and primary education in Iran. In G. Woodhill, P. B. Sakthivel, & R. Raju. (Eds.) (2006). An instrument for measuring engineering education quality from students' perspective. *The Quality Management Journal, 13*(3), 23–34.

Schwartzman, S. (1992). Non-Western societies and education. In B. R. Clark & G. Neave (Eds.), *Encyclopedia of higher education* (pp. 969–975). Oxford: Pergamon Press.

UNESCO. Institute for Statistics, "Literacy Statistics" (Retrieved March 11, 2003, from www.uis.unesco.org); United Nations Development Programme, Human Development Report 2002; UN Statistics Division, The World's Women 2000: Trends and Statistics.

UNESCO. (2003). *EFA Monitoring Report.* Published in 2003 by the United Nations Educational, Scientific and Cultural Organization, Paris. Retrieved from http://www.uis.unesco.org/Education/Documents/efa_gmr_2003-4.pdf

UNESCO Institute for Statistics. (2016). Retrieved from http://uis.unesco.org/

UNESCO United Nations Educational, Scientific and Cultural Organization. (1995). Early childhood education: Challenges and opportunities, 29. *Directory of childhood care and education organizations in the Arab states 29*, Paris, France: UNESCO.

World Bank. (1999). *Education in the Middle East and North Africa: A strategy toward learning for development.* Human Development Sector, MENA region.

World Bank. (2013). *World Development Indicators.* International Bank for Reconstruction and Development/The World Bank, Washington DC. Retrieved from http://databank.worldbank.org/data/download/WDI-2013-ebook.pdf

World Bank. (2014a). *Education in the Middle East and North Africa: New challenges.* The Syrian Crisis, MENA region.

World Bank. (2014b). *Education plays key role in advancing women, girls, and communities,* Report Says.

World Bank, World Development Indicators. (2016). International Bank for Reconstruction and Development/The World Bank, Washington DC. Retrieved from http://databank.worldbank.org/data/download/site-content/wdi-2016-highlightsfeaturing-sdgs-booklet.pdf

Young, M. E., & Mundial, B. (1996). *Early childhood development: Investing in the future.* Washington, DC: World Bank.

5

Entrepreneurs in Development: Vectors for Society's Progress

Taïeb Hafsi

Introduction

When one considers economic development, entrepreneurs appear to have a minor role to play, at least as far as policy-makers are concerned. Policy-makers would probably be more concerned about developing rules and policies that would influence economic actors' behavior, perhaps including that of entrepreneurs. Entrepreneurs are seen as adventurers, perhaps even fly-by-night and untrustworthy characters. Some seem to do well and end up wealthy. Most linger on the brink of poverty for long periods of time. They are all suspected of being potential outlaws. They are, at best, minor characters that need to be straightened out. Nobody would think of them as essential to the economic and institutional development of a country; and most thinkers or policy-makers would rather emphasize the importance of the state and its apparatus. For example,

T. Hafsi (✉)
Department of Management, HEC Montreal, Montreal, Canada

N. Azoury (ed.), *Business and Society in the Middle East*,
DOI 10.1007/978-3-319-48857-8_5

World Bank statistics rarely consider the role played by entrepreneurs, except in very general terms.

In economic theory, the market and its functioning are seen as essential institutions. Adam Smith stated that the invisible hand of the market would make the best economic decisions possible and that this would lead to economic growth. Following on from Smith, most prescriptive policy recommendations have to do with how to ensure a well-functioning or efficient market. For example, in its dealings with members, the International Monetary Fund (IMF) focuses on how the market is functioning. Most of the problems are seen as coming from impediments that hinder smooth market operations. Of course, economists are right. An efficient market is a necessary ingredient in economic development. It is the most important set of institutions in a well-functioning economy.

Yet, in his Pulitzer prize-winning book, A.D. Chandler argued that American business and economy have not been the result of the market's "invisible hand," but rather the result of the "visible hand" of entrepreneurs/managers, which led to American management culture. His conclusion was made as case studies of industries confirmed the need for proactive actors, acting within well-functioning institutions, and doing the right thing. Business entrepreneurs and managers are these necessary actors.

This was the peculiar history of America, a country where individuals and firms, in general those termed economic actors, enjoy a lot of freedom. Chandler's conclusion seems context-bound. It is hard to imagine in a different setting, especially amid turbulent institutions and where there are major constraints to business activities, that entrepreneurs/managers would have anything to do with institution-building, or even with economic development. We have started to study entrepreneurs in Algeria, an institutionally troubled country which is generally seen as hardly amicable to business, and is regularly ranked among the world's worst places to do business, to test whether Chandler's intuition about America holds in less stable environments.

In this chapter, we shall use three vignettes to describe entrepreneurial work, and to suggest that such work is not solely directed to wealth creation but also to community-building. We shall present some work patterns, then argue that they are transforming nations and building institutions. Our theory is that economic development is hardly the work of government. The best that policy-makers can do is to reduce the hurdles that states build in the path of institution-building entrepreneurs.

Benamor's Transformation of Tomato-Growing Agriculture

Amor Benamor started as a minor aspiring industrialist. His ambition was to partly substitute locally produced tomato paste for imports. Tomato paste is a basic ingredient in couscous dishes, the most important traditional meal of Algerian households. Benamor's project was not particularly welcome. First, private entrepreneurs were seen as illegitimate and money-minded bourgeois. These "parasites" were generally met with suspicion and resistance from bureaucracy. Benamor had to deal with hurdle after hurdle in order to build his plant. Second, the importers looked at the project as an attempt to reduce their hold on the business. Finally, there was a major practical problem. Tomato-growing was hard because of water consumption requirements in a generally arid countryside. As a result, the small agribusiness plant started with imported highly concentrated tomato paste and simply diluted it to manufacture a product that was familiar to Algerian households.

Sales were brisk, and as money began to flow in Benamor set his sights on dealing with tomato supply. He started asking questions and looking for solutions. The common response he received from most experts was that tomatoes could not be easily grown in his region of Algeria (Guelma). He did not believe this, and turned to advice from tomato growers in neighboring countries, in particular Spain. The answer was very different: "the land in Spain is no different from that of your region in Algeria, so tomatoes could be profitably grown." He organized international symposia, invited growers, engineers, agronomists, state administrators, and government officials, and slowly discovered and disseminated the idea that tomato-growing was possible, but that growers should use the right technology.

At these gatherings, Amor and his son Laid met an agronomist who was also a militant for dynamic agriculture. Messaoud believed that agriculture could be transformed through reasonable investment. Himself a farmer, he believed that this investment would not be made by the state but by private investors, looking for a return. He argued that if the Benamors were willing to invest, they could make money. They accepted the idea and offered to do business with Messaoud. He would be the technical guide, while they would not only invest, but also lend money, and guarantee a market and a price to all growers who would experiment with Messaoud's formula. He accepted these terms, and the project was launched.

Some farmers tried tomato-growing on small parcels of land using the new technology and achieved yields which were three to five times the traditional expectations. With the outlook even more promising, they adopted the Benamor solution. Within a few years the whole region was bubbling with tomato-growing activity, and Benamor's supply problems eased considerably. His business grew at an unbelievable pace, going from 200 tons per year to 60,000 tons within ten years.

Impressed, the ministry of agriculture approached Benamor to understand better what was going on, and was soon convinced to support the initiative. The state had been trying to do the same for 30 years, spending large amounts of money but with little success. The minister of agriculture soon became one of the strongest supporters of the Benamor formula, and asked Laid to be his advisor. As a result, Laid became influential in tomato policy-making, and he was also encouraged to set his sights on grains (wheat, barley, etc.), which were even more important as basic staples in the Algerian diet. He invested in grain-grinding, flour, and semolina- and couscous-making plants, becoming in a very short time the market leader. He was later appointed head of the regulatory body for grain growing, and went on to try and follow the same process as he had for tomatoes. This was much more difficult given the widespread wheat-growing business in Algeria, but in 2015 he was still trying. However, the minister had changed, and Laid was not benefiting from the same political support.

Overall, the whole Guelma region has been transformed. From being an importer of tomato products, Algeria was by 2015 self-sufficient and starting to export. A new philosophy was taking hold of agriculture. Growers were more numerous, and even started having difficulties finding manpower. The Guelma region, traditionally arid and brown, became green and red, with tomato-farming alive and thriving. Political officials had a new solution to stimulate agriculture, and even if their rule-making was not always appropriate and effective, Benamor and other tomato business people were listened to and encouraged. Most importantly, as mentioned above, the large wheat-growing segment has now been targeted, and there is a hope that it will go in the same direction, despite the challenges of gaining stakeholder involvement and approval.

Hasnaoui's Struggle for Sound Construction Practices and Home-Building

Brahim Hasnaoui became an entrepreneur by necessity, after losing his job as a technical civil servant. Born into a poor family in the Bel-Abbès area, a major city of Western Algeria, he was in 2016 at the helm of a major construction and land development group which has introduced important innovations in construction, and in the process contributed to changing the government's thinking about and practices in building social housing.

Hasnaoui was driven from the beginning by a desire to achieve quality building. This was soon his trademark and the source of his success. After a few general projects, he was attracted by social housing. He was convinced that he could build better housing than was currently available, even with the budgetary constraints imposed by government. He applied for a contract to build a housing complex, using a design which everyone thought was too expensive, and succeeded in building the best housing in Bel-Abbès despite the very puny budget that was allowed. Today, the "Hasnaoui housing complex" is highly valued. The apartments and houses are worth several times their initial value, and are no longer considered social housing.

Based on this experience, Hasnaoui argued with the government that housing has a critical social value. It can be the source of despair or happiness. Poor housing leads to social troubles and violence. In contrast, good housing facilitates social relationships and promotes peaceful behavior. He believed and argued that it was better to ask people to pay at least part of the cost, and to help them through loans, so as to encourage better construction. His initial proposals were adopted and became policy. Unfortunately, this has not been enforced properly. The government has being unable to face up to expressions of discontent, and has returned to distribution of de facto free housing. In so doing, it has been unable to fund construction adequately.

Despite this setback, Hasnaoui pursued his search for exemplary building formulas. His most significant achievement has been the Er-Ryad neighborhood complex. On this occasion, he decided to build regularly priced housing, to be sold to tenants without the support of the state. But in addition to building he organized the management of the neighborhood as a whole. In Er-Ryad, everything was taken into account. A police station was built. Garbage collection, internet, and TV satellite access were provided. Neighborhood improvements were undertaken, and neighborhood management was handled by a specially created management firm under the control of a tenants' association. By 2016 the Er-Ryad development was seen as a great success.

To be able to achieve the level of quality required in a poorly structured environment, Hasnaoui built a highly diversified company with several divisions, each of which dealt with an important construction function. The divisions were actually separate corporations, each run in partnership with a foreign specialist. This was designed to transfer the technology needed for good quality construction.

Hasnaoui also has a strong interest in people. He believes that they are key to success, so the training of employees is widespread. Their initiatives are valued, and the best are even encouraged to launch their own venture: Hasnaoui provides them with funding, and with the possibility to sub-contract for his group. Throughout, the emphasis is on quality and excellence.

Finally, the Hasnaoui family and group are driven by a desire to make a significant contribution to society's well-being. In addition to the drive for excellence in construction, the group encourages research, and the integration of societal values into construction. Moreover, the local community is the target for much philanthropy, to help build resilience and sustainability.

Rebrab's Push for World Competitive Industry Strategies: Being Ambitious, Starting Small, and Moving Fast

Issad Rebrab is the most notable of Algerian entrepreneurs. He started his drive soon after the country's independence. At first he was a pariah in a socialist country which had almost outlawed privately owned firms. Persistent and resilient, he succeeded in building several metal works, then a complete steel plant. His dealings in steel in the 1990s, in the midst of social violence, helped him make the break and build a cash chest. He lost his steel plant to terrorism, but the cash he had raised was used to launch his most significant venture, this time in consumer food products: Cevital.

Rebrab's strategy was fairly simple: to become competitive not only against local rivals, but also when facing strong international competition. Dealing generally in standard products (sugar, table oil, and fats), the strategy was based on economies of scale both in production and distribution. Using his experience in building plants and manufacturing facilities, he could achieve remarkably low costs. In 2016, Cevital's plants were among the largest in the world, generally exceeding the local market demand and targeting other European or African markets. Savola, a large Saudi multinational firm in table oils and fats, put Cevital to the test, building a new plant and distribution network in Western Algeria. But they could hardly make a dent in Cevital's control of the market, and by 2015 they were reeling with significant losses.

Rebrab's strategy was replicated in several other industries, in particular float glass, home appliances, home closing fixtures (doors, windows, etc.), and mass distribution. The results in these industries were mixed, forcing the company to engage in major integration strategy commitments. In particular, in 2014, the company acquired a large European home appliance company, Brandt. The strategic intent was to achieve what was called a "dual-location" strategy, which meant producing in Algeria and selling in Europe. They started to build a world-class plant in the city of Setif, thus using the Algerian advantage of low labor costs, and intended to challenge Asian and European competition in Europe.

For float glass, they also considered its integration into fixtures such as doors and windows.

What made Cevital's success was a nimble ability to move fast. Its flexibility was surprising to many. Despite its size, the company has maintained an entrepreneurial spirit, embodied in the founder and his still profound involvement in corporate management.

Like Hasnaoui, Rebrab has a keen interest in people and their well-being. He has advocated for many years that key to good people management is decent pay and respect. He has practiced these principles, and has been seen as the best employer in town by his employees. He has also systematically trained young Algerian professionals so that they can match the best in their field. For example, in the float-glass plants, he hired a Chinese company to provide coaching and training, so that company engineers could take over overall management. This they achieved in less than a year.

Finally, Rebrab does not see himself as an industrialist making money. Rather, he wants to build his country, master complex technologies, and compete with world leaders. He is constantly arguing that his compatriots should be more confident, more ambitious, and think of conquering Europe, rather than focusing on the tiny Algerian market. Consistent with this, his philanthropy is extensive, and targets universities, students, and intellectuals.

Finally, Rebrab spends liberally to help his countrymen, especially those in the poor region where he was born, to maintain old traditions and to build job-making activities.

What Do Entrepreneurs Do? Patterns of Entrepreneurial Work

The examples of Benamor, Hasnaoui, and Rebrab highlight the very constructive role of entrepreneurs in high-velocity environments. Although pursuing normal economic value creation, these entrepreneurs appear to be motivated by other deep-seated values and a concern for social-value creation.

The Maghreb in general, and Algeria in particular, have some interesting common characteristics:

1. **There is a generalized anomie**, in Durkheim's definition of the word. Anomie is characterized by an inability to build a cooperative system. According to Durkheim, "when a social system is in a state of anomie, common values and common meanings are no longer understood or accepted, and new values and meanings have not developed. According to him, such a society produces, in many of its members, psychological states characterized by a sense of futility, lack of purpose, emotional emptiness and despair" (*Encyclopedia Britannica*).
2. **External influences dominate behavior**. There is no independent thinking tradition. Most intellectuals, politicians, and professionals seem to cater to outside audiences rather than to their people. The colonial mental influence will probably last much longer than the physical occupation.
3. **There is a strong aspiration to freedom**. Probably in reaction to colonial domination, most people in the Maghreb, and much more so in Algeria, strive for a free world, in which they can realize themselves and their dreams. In turn, this leads to a generalized resistance to organized action.
4. **There is a high level of education and dissatisfaction**. Youth is a great source of energy, but also of turbulence and entropy.
5. **Initiatives are bubbling, and there is a generalized trend toward creative behavior, at least among the elite groups**. This is a source of unceasing entrepreneurial behavior in all economic, social, and political segments of society.

These characteristics suggest a need for a local outlook and a drive to build society from the grassroots. Indeed, entrepreneurs are present in the economic sector, in public administration and in general in the public sector, in social life, in cultural activities, and in politics. They are more visible in the last three because of constant contention and political strife.

The entrepreneurs described earlier highlight some important patterns, which are grouped here into five clusters:

1. Fundamentals are related to family, a morally strong founding father, little concern for money beyond basic family needs, no fear of failure and a strong, confident enthusiasm, with the belief that they will succeed.
2. In terms of achievements, they seem driven to build the best possible, to be seen as excellent, face government behavior and constraints with the desire to find solutions rather than confront. A philosophy of discretion and modest behavior.
3. Constant progress. Never stop building excellence. "We have to be among the best to convince our fellow citizens that we are worthy of their support. Take exemplary initiatives, acquire best technology, build the local know how."
4. People are important. They are a natural extension of family. Create conditions for personal development. Encourage entrepreneurial behavior. Beyond personnel, reach out to communities, building the country.
5. Very strong values, including: (1) building society and worthy projects rather than making money; (2) stimulating the country's economic and social development; (3) proposing institutional solutions to the country's problems; (4) remaining consistent with traditional values (spirituality, belief in Algeria, self-confidence, brotherhood and affection among people, work, justice, freedom); (5) remaining modest, not giving lessons to government, discretion and integrity.

Towards an Entrepreneur-Based Theory of National Competitive Advantage and Economic Growth

Economists tend to emphasize structure. How structure is designed and manipulated is seen as the key to actors' economic behavior and national economic growth. Individual actors are seen as important but they do not drive the economy. At best, they respond to economic stimuli, which are generally controlled by governments.

This view is perhaps close to reality in a stable environment, with stable institutions and clear rules laid down for the economic game. It is completely different in situations where institutions are shifting and rules are unclear. In such situations, structure is ineffective because it is forever moving. Most policy-makers see the situation as hopeless, leading to Durkheim's anomie and economic disaster.

Our observations in Algeria suggest a different perspective. Grassroots entrepreneurs work at personal survival, but in so doing they also build informal institutions and powerful rules of the game. When they succeed, they come up with initiative, innovation, and managerial behavior, all of which are attractive to young and dynamic individuals and groups. Their example becomes a powerful stimulus to more entrepreneurial behavior and ultimately growth. Chandler described the same process in the USA of the 1850s, a very dynamic society at the time.

The example that entrepreneurs give in institutionally dynamic situations highlight three basic dimensions of success:

1. A powerful ***drive for excellence***. Doing the best possible includes using the latest technology, having boundless ambitions, emulating leading competitors, and ultimately gathering the energy and courage to size them up and challenge them.
2. ***Openness and creativity***. Most entrepreneurs anywhere are innovative. Where institutions are turbulent, there is a pull to stability which hammers down any raised nails. But this is countered by an entrepreneurial push for unexpected solutions. Entrepreneurs in these situations are either completely dominated by aggressive political forces or are free, bold, and amazingly creative. However, they work hard at avoiding confrontation. In Algeria, most of them remain under the radar as long as they can.
3. Finally, strong ***progressive values*** dominate their behavior. Money is a concern only at the very beginning, where survival is a concern. As basic needs are secured, entrepreneurs move to a different plane, with high concern for people around them and concern for society. In particular, they tend to value integrity, authenticity, brotherly behavior, justice, freedom, and initiatives, and they resist bureaucratic behavior.

These three dimensions are shared by all dynamic firms that we have studied in Algeria. They contrast with firms which rely on government for survival, and are generally corruption-prone. In our study, successful entrepreneurs pointed at these "government-controlled" firms as being bound to fail. They cited at least ten examples where firms that were supported by powerful politicians ended up bankrupt or involved in major scandals.

We can therefore say that ***economic growth is the result of both structure and agency. When institutions are stable, structure dominates; when institutions are shifting, agency dominates. Entrepreneurs are the key to economic development and growth in turbulent situations*** (Hafsi, 2015).

Conclusion

The situation in Algeria is interesting. It is generating entrepreneurial behavior, which appears to play an important role in economic development and growth. Entrepreneurs are not only creating wealth; they are also building new institutions, first at the local level, then even centrally. We have argued that this behavior is particularly fruitful in those situations where institutions are in turmoil, still in contention.

The Algerian situation is in our opinion representative of what is happening in other developing and emerging economies. Our studies of some Asian and European countries show the same patterns. Furthermore, these patterns are consistent with theory, in particular strategy- and organization-based theories, which suggest the importance of agency in large and complex systems that are on the edge of chaos. But this has to be confirmed by other studies and larger samples.

The significance for policy-making is obvious. Encouraging entrepreneurial behavior is critical for economic development. This was known and clearly demonstrated in economic theory and supported by historical studies. What we see here is that this is essential in situations of institutional turbulence. Our opinion is that these situations are destructive; but entrepreneurs are the path of redemption. They should be the focus of policy, and its priority.

Bibliography

Chandler, A. (1977). *The visible hand: The managerial revolution in American business*. Cambridge, MA and London, UK: Harvard University Press.

Hafsi, T. (2015). L'Algérie et les pays du Maghreb seront probablement construits par leurs entrepreneurs. In S. Frimousse, C. Bentaleb, et al. (Eds.), *Scouarnec. Les défis du management au Maghreb*. Paris, France: Management Prospective Editions.

6

Redefining Corporate Social Responsibility

Georges Azzi and Nehme Azoury

Introduction

Corporate social responsibility (CSR) is a recently developed topic that has been discussed widely in seminars, research papers and conferences around the world. It has gained a massive reputation quickly, as it has been seen to be a way in which big companies can repent for their sins and smudge their ugly image as monsters that are trying to reap profits and increase their revenues in any way possible. This transformation has changed the view of businesses from profit-maximizing economic agents to agents with a more ethical outlook, which is aware of the impact of business on society. Globalization has imposed much pressure worldwide to enhance the image of businesses in the eyes of the public by becoming responsible citizens. Nowadays, people are becoming more educated and are starting to become aware that a healthy environment is critical to

G. Azzi • N. Azoury (✉)
USEK School of Business, Holy Spirit University of Kaslik, Jounieh, Lebanon

N. Azoury (ed.), *Business and Society in the Middle East*,
DOI 10.1007/978-3-319-48857-8_6

the welfare of human beings, now and in the future. Hence, the concept of greening management has arisen: when managers are aware that the actions of their company have an impact on the environment (Robbins et al. 2011). In other words, whenever a company is operating, it will influence its environment and surroundings. When a company becomes aware of this, its duty is to engage in green actions that reduce its negative impact, through pollution, and by helping the community more widely through investing in free education, hospitals and donations to charities. Furthermore, business ethics has become a major component of many school and university courses. Some institutions are offering courses that purely focus on business ethics and social responsibility

In today's highly interconnected digital world, managers are discovering that CSR is an important aspect of business practice. Various seminars are being organized on this topic in an attempt to create awareness and inform executives, managers and officers about recent developments and practices in the field. To many, CSR has become an important differentiator in the competitive world of business. In this context, advertising and communicating CSR practices has become a crucial aspect of marketing communication strategies. By being aware of this, companies will not only be recognized in their environment and society but will also contribute to their enhanced corporate image in the eyes of customers and the general public. All these aspects will boost a company's reputation and strengthen its brand image, and this will have an effect on financial performance and long-term profits.

Instilling a Culture of Social Responsibility in the Arab World

In the Middle East, the accepted cultural mores imply that wealth and profit-making is important to determine one's status and position in society. It is well known that corruption and unethical practices are widely present in the private as well as in the public sector, which is mostly due to minimal government intervention and control. This explains why the concept of CSR is still in its very early phases of development in the Arab world. Nowadays, with the rise of social media and the development of education in this area, more people are starting to be aware of the issue. Some international corporations that are operating in the Arab region have already started implementing various CSR initiatives, while local companies are beginning to follow suit.

In the Middle East, religion plays a major role in Arab culture and in the business world alike. The two dominant religions in the region are Islam and Christianity, and both deem it essential to help the poor and the needy. Charity has a major impact on people's lives in the Middle East since many religious texts encourage public good and charitable activities. In Islam, the concept of Zakat implies giving a portion of one's wealth to people in need, while in Christianity it is highly recommended that a person should help disadvantaged people, especially during the Christmas and Easter periods.

Most of the companies in the region, and especially in Lebanon, are family owned. Therefore, we can deduce that the application of CSR in Arab companies is mainly related to the religious upbringing of business owners. If an owner has a strong religious affiliation, he will integrate its principles with the company's vision and mission, which will be dictated thereafter by senior management. However, if the business owner is not a true believer, he might see CSR as unwarranted expense, and might prefer to invest in other areas that will have a direct and quick impact on company performance. In reality, CSR must be implemented regardless of whatever the owner thinks, as it has a business and professional connotation rather than a religious connotation.

Application of CSR and Its Major Types

When we think of CSR it involves thinking about the multiple responsibilities that the company has towards multiple stakeholders. There are four areas that need to be considered which form a pyramid: these are economic, legal, ethical and philanthropic responsibilities (Carroll 1991).

Economic responsibility is considered to be the base of the pyramid, indicating that financial viability and profit are essential for the company's survival. One of the major proponents of this view was Milton Friedman, who argued that management's sole responsibility is to maximize profits to shareholders. He also likened managers to thieves who are trying to distribute what is not theirs. This action can be considered to be an illegitimate exercise of power, since the money invested in CSR is considered to be a lost investment which should instead be added to the shareholders' wealth. In Friedman's opinion money such as that invested in CSR does not benefit the organization and represents a cost: the only liability that the managers have is towards the shareholders, who have entrusted their wealth to them.

Legal responsibility is the second component. According to this, the business must be conducted according to the laws of the country in which it is operating. Laws may differ from one place to another and might change over time. They are the minimum standard that businesses need to conform to, or else they will be penalized or fined by the government and legal institutions.

Ethical responsibilities go beyond duties and obligations to do the right thing. They rely on the ethical understanding and culture of the company decision-makers. This responsibility represents a major challenge for managers, especially when they are confronted with an ethical dilemma or when they need to incur extra costs on their company in order to preserve the environment, protect the health of their employees or manufacture safe products for customers. All these decisions can put managers' ethics and a company's profits on the line. The right course of action is always to align an organization's benefits with environmental practices and society's needs.

The ultimate level of CSR in the pyramid is the philanthropic responsibility that promotes human welfare. This includes donations of products, services, time or money to the community. It is considered a voluntary action, and many large companies have established foundations to handle this process. For instance, Bill Gates, the co-founder of Microsoft, and his wife gave away 95% of their wealth and established a multi-billion dollar foundation that focuses on health issues, namely AIDS, malaria and tuberculosis (Treviño and Nelson 2014). Those types of actions stem from strong beliefs and a deep organizational culture which deems that doing public good and improving society's well-being is the right thing to do. The donators in this case do not expect a return for their efforts or their money invested in this manner, since they truly believe that this is the right thing to do (Fig. 6.1).

Fig. 6.1 Corporate Social Responsibility Pyramid. Adapted from Archie B. Carroll, The Pyramid of Corporate Social Responsibility: Toward the Moral Management of Organizational Stakeholders, *Business Horizons*, July, August, 1991, pp. 39–48

Businesses Cannot Transform Overnight to Be Perfectly Socially Responsible Organizations

As Zadek (2004) states, most businesses pass through five stages to develop a sense of responsibility and to take actions as corporate citizens. The first stage is the "defensive stage," where the company is criticized for its actions by customers, media, investors and other stakeholders. As a result, the company tends to reject and deny the accusations that are made mainly through responses and statements initiated by the legal and communication departments. The company's only concern is short-term sales and profits, and the long-term effects of its actions are disregarded. The second stage is the "compliance stage," whereby the company responds to its critics through managerial actions. Extra costs are incurred as the company protects its brand image and limits the risk of legal lawsuits. The third stage is the "managerial stage," which takes place when the company realizes that compliance is not sufficient to deal with the general public. In this stage, managers are creative in finding long-term solutions and responsible practices that will become an integral part of the company's mindset and strategy. In the fourth stage, the "strategic stage," managers integrate societal strategies and concentrate on them to add value and to give an edge over their competitors in the long run. During the last stage, the "civil stage," the company supports massive initiatives that support community concerns and society needs. Some companies also think about how their future role and presence will affect society.

Hence, whether the company is still in its early stages or in the most developed ones depends on numerous factors such as public pressure, competition, the culture within the organization, and the strength of the role of media and government.

Impact on Community, Environment and Organizational Performance

In general, CSR tries to explain and make evident the extent of the social and economic role of a business in society. Thus in its broader context, it takes into consideration the impact of the actions of the organization on all its stakeholders. Thus, we can consider that CSR is a stakeholder approach that focuses on the voluntary actions and commitments of an organization that is targeted towards internal and external issues that determine an understanding and awareness of its moral responsibilities with regard to society (Maon et al. 2010).

The blessing of the community is considered to be an important factor in organizational performance. A company cannot survive if it has bad relations with the surrounding community, the community playing the role of a powerful stakeholder that can either promote the company's reputation and profits or bring about its demise. Therefore, caring for people ranks high in organizations that are fulfilling their CSR initiatives. A company doing business cannot easily oversee its impact on the overall stakeholders, so for a corporation to survive and grow it has to work closely with the surrounding community and receive its endorsement through creating meaningful dialogues and successful initiatives that have a direct impact on people's lives. At employee level, workers are treated fairly and equally while maintaining safe and comfortable working conditions, perhaps enjoying a periodic medical check.

At customer level, the company will be producing or using safe products that are free from all defects or any substance that may affect negatively their health.

The environment is considered to be probably one of the most important aspects of CSR. Companies can indirectly affect the environment in many different ways. Companies use electricity, some manufacturing companies dispatch polluted air into the atmosphere or infected or unfiltered water in the ocean, while others use up the earth's natural resources. As a way to pay back these costs, companies engage in green activities: they plant trees, use renewable sources of energy and recycle paper, among many other activities that help to preserve the environment and limit the excessive degradation of the earth's non-renewable resources.

By committing to such initiatives, the company's positioning and image will improve, employees' motivation and engagement will increase and they will start believing in the company's mission towards the society and environment. In addition, customers who are becoming more sensitive and aware about CSR will appreciate the company's actions and this may affect their loyalty. On top of this, positive word of mouth may be generated in the local community about such actions, a sincere commitment to support humanitarian and social causes resulting in a trustworthy reputation.

New Actions Towards a Better Tomorrow

In order to guarantee a better tomorrow, it is fundamental to promote a future generation which is raised on the basics of ethics and sustainability through the instilling and strengthening of the ideology of CSR. This process starts at school and continues to secondary and tertiary education. The children are the seeds of the future, and if we put them on the right track we will have a bright outlook. Hence, integrating CSR mentality into education and instilling this culture at school is quite important since it will be deeply rooted in their culture and behavior as they grow up. At university level, it is important to hone the practices and ethical spirit at a professional level, so that when students graduate and gain professional positions in the business world, they will be leading their institutions with integrity, honesty and high levels of ethical conduct. Some of the Middle Eastern higher education institutions, especially in Lebanon, have started to integrate topics in different courses that focus on environmental sustainability and managerial ethics. Students will be prepared to tackle real world problems by solving ethical dilemmas. This is considered the most effective academic procedure: learning by doing and putting theory into practice.

The importance of implementing CSR initiatives in the region has led non-governmental organizations and associations to reward companies that adhere and apply CSR to their organizations. Nowadays, Arab governments have started a new policy of supporting campaigns that raise awareness about CSR and tend to exempt or in some cases reduce taxes for those companies who are applying CSR practices. Yearly awards recognize companies who have invested and implemented CSR initiatives which have had an impact on their surroundings.

For instance, CSR Levant awards entrepreneurial initiatives, establishes solid partnerships, develops impactful CSR strategies and empowers the next generation. CSR Lebanon (www.csrlebanon.com) raises awareness about CSR, aiming to provide a better understanding of the concept in the private and public sectors and among the community as a whole.

In this context many forums and online platforms are evolving, such as Arabia CSR Network (www.arabiacsrnetwork.com). This is a professional multi-stakeholder organization which is devoted to promoting the principles of CSR in the region. It encourages and recognizes responsible business practices through services and other offerings, including training, research and best practice, advisory services, third party assurance and a Pan-Arab acclaimed award initiative known as the Arabia CSR Awards.

CSR Middle East (www.csrmiddleeast.org) is a professional non-profit platform and the regional source and network for CSR and sustainability in the Middle East. It promotes corporate social responsibility in the region based upon the sharing of CSR updates, solutions and shaping modern businesses. Its mission is "to help companies achieve profitability, sustainable growth and human progress by placing corporate social responsibility in the mainstream of business practice."

Conclusion

In light of the rapid changes that the world is witnessing, we cannot just remain spectators. The time has come for us to define the future for the upcoming generation before everything is lost. The environment is an asset inherited from our ancestors, and it is our duty and responsibility to preserve it and sustain it for the future. Therefore the role and concept of social responsibility should be integrated into every business and educational institution. The time has come to shift from managerial ethics and high levels of corporate social responsibility being an option to an obligation. This involves protecting and sustaining natural resources, protecting the life and health of employees, taking actions and creating initiatives that enhance the quality of life of the community. Whenever corporations commit to CSR, it is an effective way of achieving brand loyalty, a solid reputation and goodwill among a range of different stakeholders. CSR practice is also the best way in which to win the hearts of both employees and customers, and transparent business practices and proper management of responsible business practices together with effective management of the company's resources can improve organizational performance in the long run.

Our faith in our region is immense, and many initiatives are beginning, yet our role as educational institutions and businesses is central in the change process from blind profit-making to responsible actions that sustain the environment and evolve into an ethical mindset that involves CSR towards different stakeholders. A new concept is arising among members of the corporate community who are going beyond core business operations and seeing themselves as the main vehicles for social change. Finally, with the support of social enterprises, small and medium-sized enterprises, academics, law-makers, non-governmental organizations and associations, hand in hand they can create an ecosystem that will support long-term, sustainable initiatives that will have considerable social impact.

Bibliography

Carroll, A. (1991). The pyramid of corporate social responsibility: Toward the moral management of organizational stakeholders. *Business Horizons*, July–August, pp. 39–48.

Maon, F., Lindgreen, A., & Swaen, V. (2010). Organizational stages and cultural phases: A critical review and a consolidative model of corporate social responsibility development. *International Journal of Management Reviews, 12*(1), 20–38.

Robbins, S. P., Coulter, M., Sidani, Y., & Jamali, D. (2011). *Management* (Arab World ed.). Essex, UK: Pearson Education Limited.

Treviño, L., & Nelson, K. (2014). *Managing business ethics—Straight talk about how to do it right* (6th ed.). Hoboken, NJ: John Wiley and Sons.

www.arabiacsrnetwork.com

www.csrlebanon.com

www.csrmiddleeast.org

Zadek, S. (2004). The Path to Corporate Social Responsibility. In *Harvard Business Review on Point Collection (2007)*, 36–44. Harvard Business School Publishing Corporation.

7

The Impact of Businesses in the MENA Region

Thami Ghorfi and Imad Eddine Hatimi

Introduction

The MENA region (Middle East and North Africa) is the source of growth prospects at the economic level; however, it faces a disparity of resources and a global context that although increasingly competitive is marked by instability.[1] This has resulted in a slowdown in foreign direct investment (FDI) and exports (Morocco, Jordan, etc.) and lower domestic revenues (Algeria, Saudi Arabia, etc.). According to UNDP (2014),[2] the growth of gross national income (GNI) per capita has declined in the MENA region. Finally, corruption and the informal sector are still hampering the economic growth of the countries in the region.

[1] The MENA region encompasses the following countries: Algeria, Saudi Arabia, Bahrain, West Bank and Gaza, Djibouti, Egypt, United Arab Emirates, Iran, Iraq, Jordan, Kuwait, Lebanon, Libya, Malta, Morocco, Oman Sultanate, Qatar, Syria, Tunisia, Yemen.

[2] United Nations Development Program.

T. Ghorfi (✉) • I.E. Hatimi
ESCA Ecole de Management, ESCA, Casablanca, Morocco

N. Azoury (ed.), *Business and Society in the Middle East*,
DOI 10.1007/978-3-319-48857-8_7

In geopolitical terms, the MENA region is experiencing significant changes following the Arab Spring revolutions. Several countries are victims of armed conflicts (Iraq, Libya, Syria and Yemen) or national or regional political instability leading to investment flight and an influx of refugees (Egypt, Jordan, Lebanon, Tunisia, etc.). The instability created by the concomitant development of the armed groups of Daesh increases tensions within the region's societies, and make the situation and therefore analysis of it even more complex.

Such events have made the precarious living conditions of the population of these countries worse; the unemployment rate has reached worrying numbers and social services are sorely lacking in most countries and insufficient in others. Finally, the infrastructure is becoming increasingly dilapidated.

Consequently, the MENA countries are lagging behind in terms of human development index. In fact, the deterioration in the purchasing power of the workforce, increasing disparities among social classes and in terms of gender, along with youth marginalization, cannot but be noted. Indeed, these countries need sustained growth to meet challenges in terms of creating jobs for a demographically dominant young population. They also need investment in infrastructure and social services.

In this context, the expectations of the people and societies of the region, in their diversity, are even higher towards the states, governors and economic actors. This chapter aims to show the role that companies in the MENA region can play; they are called, in fact, to enable their countries to address these economic and societal challenges. To this end, companies that have managed to create value in their context and emerge as national and sometimes regional champions will be studied.

The chapter is composed of three sections. The first recalls the main economic and social stakes in the MENA region, while the second focuses on solutions that have been proposed to allow the region's countries to meet these challenges. The third section is interested in models and practices developed by companies in these societies in order to support the implementation of their development strategies. In this context, cases in

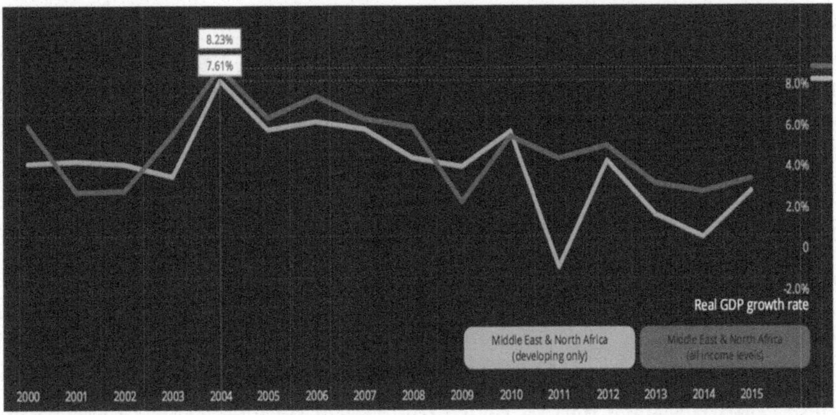

Fig. 7.1 The Evolution of the GDP growth rate in the MENA region

Moroccan companies are used to illustrate the proposed solutions and the associated impact at economic and societal levels.

The MENA Region: Serious Socio-Economic Challenges

The MENA region includes a great diversity of countries in terms of political, economic and social structures. Included in this region are monarchist and republican regimes, countries considered as oil exporters and importers, cultures under Anglo-Saxon influence and French-speaking cultures, fully Arab societies and others with a mix of Arab-Berbers, Asians and other African, and different religious affiliations despite the Muslim dominance, which is itself diverse in terms of religious trends.

Despite this, the MENA countries face similar challenges in terms of human development. Generally, a vulnerable economy and precarious social conditions may be noted here.

A Vulnerable Economy:

In recent years, the MENA region has been experiencing a slowdown in economic growth at the global level (Fig. 7.1). In fact, while the average growth rate of real gross domestic product (GDP) was higher than 8% at the beginning of 2004, the region has witnessed a growth slowdown, in some cases to no growth at all (World Bank 2016a). Since 2011, the economic situation has deteriorated because of the upheavals of the Arab Spring. According to the IMF (2015a), the International Monetary Fund, the average growth rate was around 2.6% in 2015 and should increase in 2016 to be closer to 4%. Figure 7.1 shows the evolution of the GDP growth rate in the MENA region, according to the World Bank (2016a).

In this sense, the fall in oil prices was a blow to some countries in the MENA region and particularly to those for whom it represents a significant financial windfall (Algeria, Saudi Arabia, etc.). Consequently, these countries have had to revise their fiscal policies. These restrictions have affected their non-oil activities and have slowed government spending, therefore reducing employment opportunities in the public sector. If such a fall in oil prices was to continue, it would lead to budget deficits ranging from 4% in Algeria to 8% in the Gulf countries. This is important if we take into account that in some countries the Arab Spring has been contained by an increase in payrolls and a deliberate unemployment absorption policy.

With regard to the MENA region oil importers, the oil price fall has enabled them to improve their external revenues. Cases in point are Morocco, Lebanon and Mauritania. This does not in itself improve their economic situation, and it may be seen that exports are not growing fast enough. It is worth mentioning that perceived insecurity in the region scares away foreign investment funds and encourages them to resort to other parts of the world.

In terms of exports, according to the World Bank (2016b), the countries in the MENA region have experienced a decline since 2012 when they used to account for 52% of GDP, reaching 47.3% in 2014. As for imports, they increased within the same period by 6.5%. We should also note that the exported MENA products are in general of low added value. Exports emanating from technological transformation in the MENA region (in areas such as aerospace, computers, pharmaceuticals, electrical machinery and scientific instruments) only represent 0.7% of the total of world exports in this category.[3] In 2009, they were only 3.4%

[3] Products that have benefited from major R&D activity.

of exported manufactured goods, which is around six times less than the world average.

In terms of FDI, according to the World Bank (2016b), the MENA region attracted, in 2014, US $50 billion (3% of the total of FDI), which is a decrease of 60% compared to 2008, when it represented US $123 billion (6% of the total of FDI). Between 2010 and 2013, sub-Saharan Africa and Latin America and the Caribbean increased their FDI by 60% and 66% respectively, in contrast to the MENA region which experienced a 40% drop. Moreover, such investments are generally oriented towards the natural resources sector (gas, oil, etc.) according to FDI Intelligence (2014), which limits their economic impact in terms of job creation and technology transfer.

Furthermore, the economic situation in the MENA region is also due to its lack of attractiveness and competitiveness. Indeed, and except for Oman, Morocco, Tunisia, Qatar and the United Arab Emirates (UAE), all the other countries in the region occupy between 77 and 188 in the 2016 Doing Business Ranking (World Bank 2016c), with an index average of 111 for the region. According to a recent study led by the European Bank for Reconstruction and Development (2015) on the companies in this region, corruption and the informal economy, in addition to political instability, were the major obstacles.

Indeed, the MENA region is characterized by a business climate marked by mistrust because of corruption and the informal economy. According to Transparency International (2015), the Corruption Perception Index in the public sector in most countries in the region is less than 40. They are grouped in the second half of the World Bank ranking, which reflects a high corruption rate in the public sector. According to the estimates of the World Bank, such a phenomenon would cost the economy of the country 1–1.5 points of growth, and about 22% of the companies mentioned that they had informally paid public officials for administrative services.

Moreover, the economy in the MENA region suffers from the negative influence on the business climate and enterprise competitiveness of the informal sector. The percentage of MENA companies considering the informal sector as a major constraint to their competitiveness has reached 31.4, as opposed to 14.5 in OECD (Organisation for Economic

Co-operation and Development) countries, according to a survey by the World Bank.[4] In 2010, the shadow economy accounted for about 27.2% of GDP and 67% of the workforce was not declared to social security (Loayza and Wada 2010). It employs two-thirds of the working population, including a significant portion without qualifications. Such a phenomenon is related to the level of entrepreneurs' education and taxation conditions in these countries.

In addition, the economy of the MENA region remains relatively dependent on its natural resources. On one hand, the wealth of some of the countries is based on oil and gas and is therefore susceptible to world price volatility. On the other hand, in 2013 the agricultural sector in the MENA region contributed to 6.4% of GDP (10% for developing countries in the area), which is twice the global average (3.1). This is noteworthy if one takes into account that only 4.7% of the lands in the area were cultivated in 2013 compared with 10.9% as the world average (World Bank 2016b). The rest is mainly composed of desert areas. In addition, access to water is limited in the MENA region, since it has only 1% of natural water resources for a population that represents 4.25% of the world population (World Bank 2016b). According to the World Economic Forum (2010), internal renewable freshwater resources per capita are estimated as 565 m^3 in the MENA region, as opposed to 6013.2 m^3 as the world average. Consequently, the economic situation in several countries depends on climatic conditions, specifically rainfall.

Finally, the economic situation in the region is exacerbated by the armed conflicts prevailing in some countries (Iraq, Libya, Syria and Yemen), which have a negative impact on neighboring countries; the latter are in fact witnessing a massive flow of refugees to Lebanon, Jordan, Tunisia and Egypt. According to the Institute for Economics and Peace (2015), the MENA region is facing its worst situation since 2008, and is currently considered the most violent region of the world. Increasing uncertainty in the region has had a direct economic impact on tourism and investments in general (in the case of Tunisia, Egypt and Turkey). Table 7.1 reports the human damage and the costs associated to armed conflicts in some countries of the MENA region.

[4] http://www.enterprisesurveys.org/Data/ExploreTopics/informality.

Table 7.1 Key conflict statistics for countries profiled, 2014

Country	Conflict-related fatalities	Total displaced persons	Internally displaced persons (IDPs)	Refugees originating from the country	Foreign refugees residing in the country	Cost of violence (US $)	Cost as % of GDP (%)
Syria	71,667	9,550,265	6,520,800	3,029,465	149,377	$56,736,469,736	42
Iraq	18,489	2,330,057	1,903,943	426,114	254,215	$152,322,962,059	31
Yemen	3836	337,026	334,512	2514	245,801	$9,951,422,174	9
Libya	3060	67,338	63,985	3353	25,561	$14,673,899,539	14
Israel[a]	2414	1043	0	1043	48,201	$32,214,622,557	12
Lebanon	360	4238	0	4238	1,115,988	$6,646,573,618	8

Source: IEP and Office of the United Nations High Commissioner for Refugees

[a]Not including Palestine; according to the BADIL Resource Centre 6.8 million Palestinian refugees and 519,000 IDPs have been displaced since 1949

Precarious Social Conditions

Given its economic and geopolitical conditions, the MENA region is facing major challenges at the social level. According to UNDP (2015), the Arab countries,[5] despite the oil resources of some of them, had a human development index of 0.686 (against a maximum value of 1). This positions the region in third place after Europe/Central Asia and East Asia/the Pacific. This is explained by the problems in terms of standards of living, gender equity and social services.

First of all, the GDP income per capita in the MENA region has experienced a decline since 2012, contrary to the upward trend noted at global level (World Bank 2016b). The average gross national income in the region is growing less than that seen on a global scale, particularly in developing countries in this area. It was around US $8697.80 in 2013 across the whole region and only $4722.40 in the developing countries, which is below the global average of US $10,720.

MENA countries also faced a high unemployment rate of around 11.3% in 2014, compared to 5.9% worldwide (World Bank 2016b). In addition, in 2012, precarious employment represented 30.7% of total employment. Such problems particularly affect young people and women.

In fact, the participation rate in the workforce of young people aged 15 and 24 was only 32.4% compared to 47.3% worldwide (World Bank 2016b). This is particularly important if we take into account that the population of the MENA region is characterized by a young population, with over two-thirds being under 30 years old. A young population is promising in that it supports growth in the region, but it brings with it a strong need for social development, and is the source of universal aspirations for human rights. Unfortunately, owing to the region's weak economic growth, the unemployment rate affects disproportionate numbers of the youth. Moreover, the political systems in place do not promote enough youth participation in public life. It is also worth mentioning that it was mainly these young people, animated by the desire to achieve their goals, who were behind the popular uprisings that have

[5] The MENA region is mainly composed of Arab countries.

shaken the country. Social networks were their vehicles; they also take refuge online in order to build dreams and have influence on their environments. Otherwise, some will empower terrorist groups such as Daesh and Al-Qaeda.

Furthermore, gender appears to be a major challenge in the MENA region. Unemployment affects women more than men, for example: in 2014, 20.5% of the female workforce was unemployed, as opposed to 8.8% of men. In addition, women's participation in paid economic activities is limited (16.2% in 2014 against 38.9% globally), and female employment is suffering from insecurity (35.4% as a percentage of vulnerable employment in 2012) (World Bank 2016b). Senior positions are dominated by men. Indeed, only 5.6% of the MENA companies were headed by women in 2015, as opposed to 22.1% in the Eurozone and 17.4% worldwide (World Bank 2016b).

It should be recalled that according to the report of the World Bank (2015), Women, Business and Law 2016, the lack of participation of women in professional activities and entrepreneurship results to a loss of 27% of income in the MENA region. Hence, the promotion of women's employment is essential. Women are more likely to access education and particularly higher education. In some countries in the region, women cannot claim access to employment without the prior approval of their husband or guardian. This is the situation they are facing in Bahrain, Jordan, Kuwait, Mauritania, Qatar, Sudan, the UAE and Yemen. In this context, various obstacles to women's access to employment in the region are noted; they are systematically discriminated against. There is much to do.

Thus, the MENA region countries occupy the last positions in the ranking of the 2015 "Global Gender Gap" of the World Economic Forum (2015). The last 20 countries of the ranking list are MENA countries, also half of the 145 countries on the list are also MENA countries, more than half of them come from this area, knowing that Iraq, Palestine and Libya were not on the list. Therefore, the MENA region achieves the lowest progress in gender equity, compared with 2006. Only 40% of the gap has been filled, with an increase of 1%. Consequently, these disparities between men and women are shown especially in terms of their participation in economic activities, and do not seem to be reducing.

Besides, the problems of education and health that hinder the development of the MENA region countries are to be considered as well. According to UNDP (2015), individuals' satisfaction with the quality of education and health care in the Arab countries is lower than that observed in all other regions of the world.

First, access to health care is still lagging, which makes it important for the countries of the MENA region to deploy substantial efforts at this level (World Bank 2016b). Expenses reserved for health care (4.7% of GDP) are lower than the world average (10%). This health care weakness is more obvious when it comes to spending per capita (US $403 in the MENA region, versus US $1041 as a world average). This sheds light on the low level of aid provided to the people of the region in terms of health services (preventive and curative), family planning, activities related to nutrition and emergency aid reserved for health. Figure 7.2 shows the evolution of spending on health per capita in the world and in the MENA region, according to data from the World Bank (2016b).

Second, despite the progress made in recent years, schooling remains a major issue. On one hand, according to UNDP (2015), only 40% of the population of Arab countries had at least a high school education in 2015. On the other hand, the average years spent at school in Arab

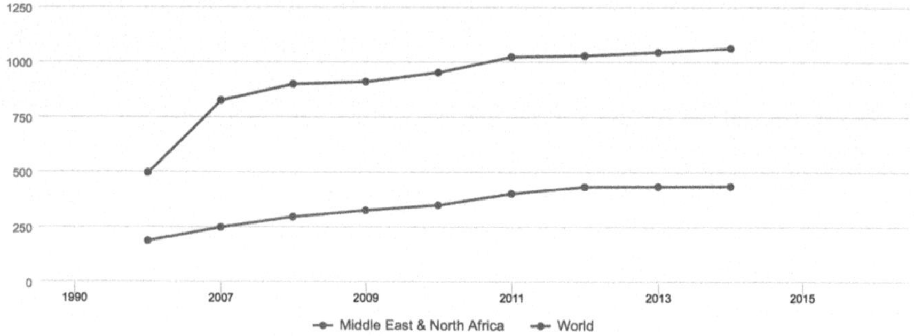

Fig. 7.2 The evolution of expenses related to health services

countries is estimated as 6.4 as opposed to 10 in Europe and Central Asia. The gap created is even more obvious if we take into account that one year of education increases the individual income of the child by 10%. Moreover, the quality of education is at stake in the MENA countries. In fact, according to the results of TIMSS Mathematics in 2011, students are below international standards. In addition, 40% of Arab companies report a lack of human resources skills as a major obstacle to their growth.

Such social conditions are even more alarming when one considers the demographic and cultural development of societies in the MENA region. Indeed, despite the slowdown in the birth rate observed in recent years, the population in the countries in this region will experience strong growth. In 2014, there were 394.1 million people, with an annual growth of about 2% compared to 1.2% as the world average (World Bank 2016b). This trend should continue, according to United Nations projections (2007), and this will in particular affect the Arabian Peninsula (Fig. 7.3).

The MENA region is also experiencing a cultural transformation with the opening of its population to the international scene, following the

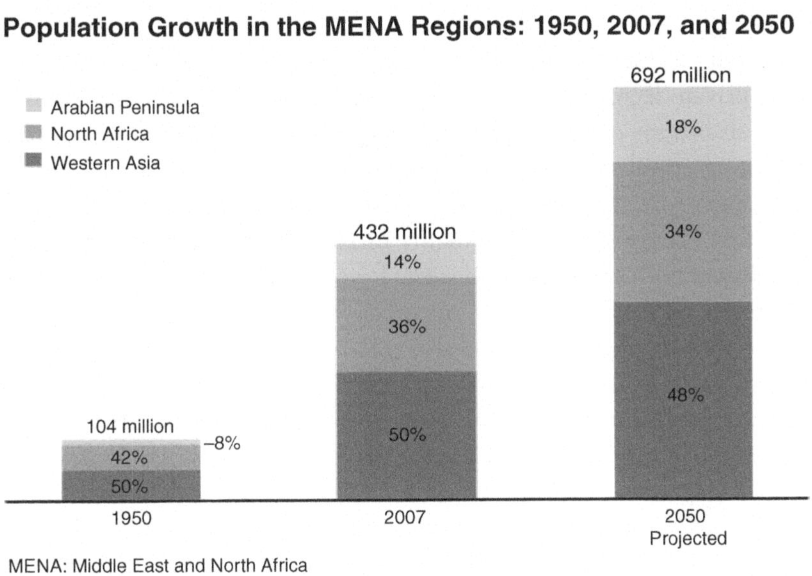

Fig. 7.3 Demographic evolution until 2050 in the MENA region

introduction of new technologies and the mobility of people across countries. The accessibility of social networks and, more broadly, the Internet, has enabled people to discover the cultural diversity of the world and to forge universal aspirations for freedom and progress. This trend was initiated by satellite TV and telephone: in 2014, the average of telephone subscribers for every 100 people was 110.6, compared to 96.3 in the world. In 2015, 52% of the MENA region population was using the Internet, a higher rate than reported in the rest of the world (46.2%).[6] In Morocco, the number of phone users was higher than the number of potential voters. In 2016, about 20% of the population of the MENA region accessed social networks, with an annual growth of 2%.[7] Moreover, the mobility of people across countries has contributed to the mixing of cultures, allowing a gradual globalization of MENA companies' values, but not without internal friction.

The Private Sector as a Key to Competitiveness in the MENA Region: The Case of Morocco

That being said, it is clear that with the significant social and economic challenges that characterize the MENA region, economic policies must focus on the private sector to generate economic growth that will create enough jobs to absorb the existing unemployment and meet the needs of a particularly young population. With 2.8 million young people entering the labor market each year, the region's economy cannot be based only on the public sector that is currently predominant. In fact, the major challenges facing the region at both economic and social levels require a strong private sector.

In order to understand the necessary strategies for addressing these socio-economic challenges and the role of private companies, the case of Morocco is an interesting case in point. It is enough, in this scope, to study the evolution of its GDP per capita and its human development index in the last decades in which the private sector has played an important role (Figs. 7.4 and 7.5).

In fact, Morocco has experienced macroeconomic stability with an average growth of around 5% since 2000 and controlled inflation (1.3%

[6] http://www.internetworldstats.com/stats5.htm.

[7] http://www.statista.com/statistics/244925/social-network-penetration-in-the-middle-east-and-africa/.

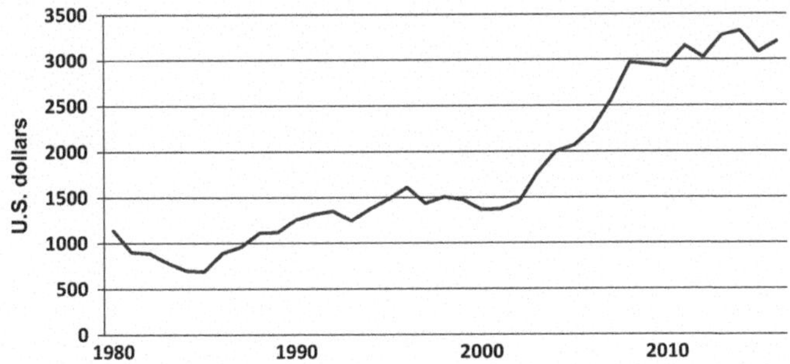

Fig. 7.4 The evolution of the GDP per capita in Morocco (http://perspective.usherbrooke.ca/bilan/servlet/BMTendanceStatPays?codeTheme=2&codeStat=NY.GDP.PCAP.KD&codePays=MAR&codeTheme2=7&codeStat2=x&codePays2=MAR&langue=fr)

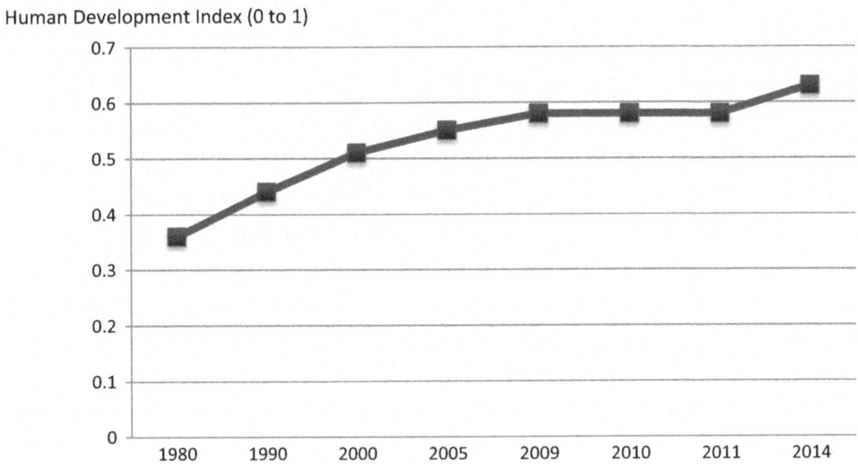

Fig. 7.5 The evolution of the human development index in Morocco (http://perspective.usherbrooke.ca/bilan/servlet/BMTendanceStatPays?codeTheme=1&codeStat=SP.POP.IDH.IN&codePays=MAR&codeTheme2=7&codeStat2=x&codePays2=MAR&langue=fr)

in 2012). Since the end of the Structural Adjustment Programme (SAP) to 2016, Morocco's GDP has tripled. This is owing to various reforms that have been carried out and an economic diversification process adopted by the Government to reduce deficits, increase productivity and improve the country's attractiveness to foreign investments. Thus, according to IMF

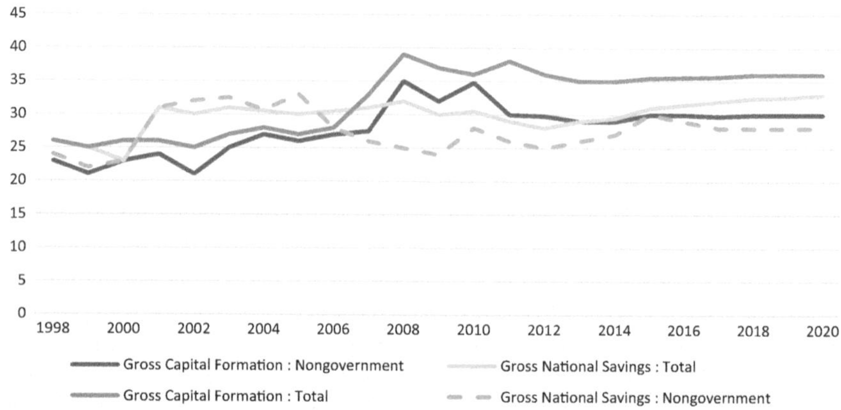

Fig. 7.6 The evolution of the private capital contribution percentage to national investments in Morocco

(2015b) estimates, Morocco should benefit from a growth of around 4.5 to 5.8% between 2013 and 2018.

Such a development is due in part to the private sector, which since 2013 has been witnessing a positive dynamic. According to the IMF (2015b), this sector represented 30% of the GDP over the last five years; however, given the importance of the informal sector in Morocco, some estimates give higher rates of around 45% of total investments (Fig. 7.6).[8]

This is particularly important if we take into account that, according to IMF (2015b), such a development depends increasingly on an industrialized economy (Fig. 7.7).

In order to promote the development of its private sector, Morocco has followed the recommendations of the World Bank (2008):

- The improvement of the regulatory and administrative framework of the economy, to facilitate the entry and exit of private enterprises, support their growth and encourage free competition;
- The support of private enterprises by facilitating access to financing for the purposes of launching and operation;
- The provision of private lands and necessary infrastructure needed for better trade logistics;

[8] http://lavieeco.com/news/economie/linvestissement-prive-en-perte-de-vitesse.html.

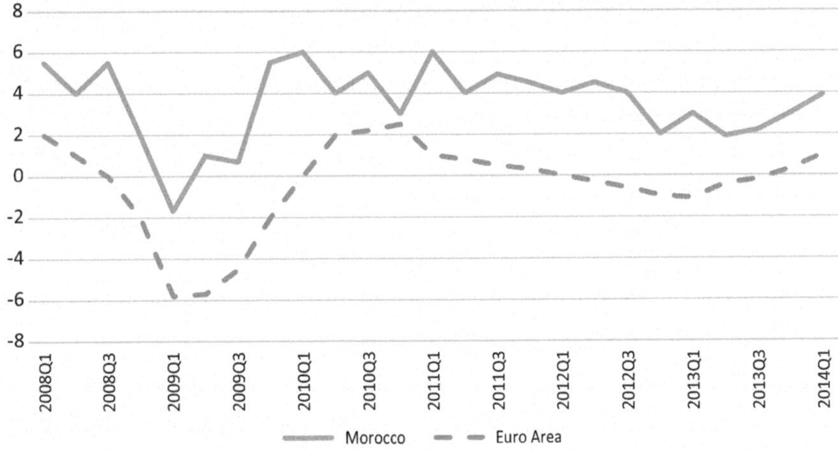

Fig. 7.7 The evolution of the growth rates of the non-agricultural sector (OECD (2016))

- The reduction of state intervention in the economy, by developing public/private partnerships.

Since the end of the SAP Morocco has conducted several reforms,[9] thus increasing the country's productivity and improving the attractiveness of foreign investments, namely:

- Reform of public/private partnerships and public markets;
- Liberalization of some sectors such as health;
- Reform of the investment charter with a view to strengthening incentives and simplifying legal and administrative aspects;
- Justice reform to strengthen the fight against corruption and money laundering;
- Reform of industrial property to improve the protection of intellectual property;
- Strengthening of the Competition Council to promote free, fair and transparent competition;
- Reform of the banking and financial sector to facilitate access to finance national enterprises, while strengthening legal certainty for

[9] https://www.dlapiper.com/fr/morocco/insights/publications/2015/12/liberal-reforms-in-morocco/.

lenders and enriching the financing offer through the banks' participation;
- Reform of the stock market to facilitate access to capital markets for a larger number of enterprises;
- Reform of firms in difficulty to ensure the rights of both debtors and creditors;
- Reform of special training contracts to improve the productivity of small and medium-sized enterprises (SMEs);
- Reform of the mining code to streamline prospecting licenses and their enlargement.

Secondly, Morocco has taken several actions to improve the business environment through better infrastructure (38 ports including Tangier-Med which is the largest in Africa; 24 airports, with the largest in Western Africa serving 30 continental destinations; and a network of highways over 2000 km) and strong competitiveness in terms of cost, proximity and size of the market (free trade agreements with 55 countries already giving access to a market of 1 billion consumers). Such efforts have enabled Morocco to become one of the most attractive countries in Africa and the MENA region (sixth), according to the Doing Business 2016 ranking of the World Bank, with the 75th spot out of 189 countries, compared to 114th spot in 2011 (World Bank 2016c).

In parallel with this, Morocco is experiencing development based on sector strategies: the Industrial Plan for Acceleration, which is aimed at integrating Morocco into a number of global businesses (such as automotive, aerospace, offshoring and textiles), the 2020 Vision for Tourism, the Halieutis Plan for sea products development and the Agricultural Green Morocco Plan. This last seeks to reduce the share of traditional agriculture in the GDP, through its modernization in two ways: aggregation to intensify agricultural production and strengthening the transformation of agricultural products by supporting the development of the food industry.

More specifically, Morocco has launched in recent years a National Pact for Industrial Emergence.[10] This was established between the state and the private sector, and aims to guide Moroccan industry players towards

[10] http://www.emergence.gov.ma/Pacte/Documents/PACTE.pdf.

sectors where Morocco has competitive advantages. Among these sectors, we can mention the offshoring, automotive, aerospace, electronics, food processing, and textile and leather sectors. This strategy was extended by the Industrial Acceleration Plan (2014–2020), which has set the goals of generating 23% of GDP through industrial sectors and the creation of 500,000 jobs.

In a similar vein, Morocco has supported the policy of exports and FDI. Regarding exports, the economy has experienced significant benefits since the country's accession to the World Trade Organization (WTO) in 1995 and the signing of several free trade agreements with the European Union, the USA and many other countries, especially in Africa. Thus, the opening rate of the national economy rose from 51% in 2000 to 64.8% in 2011, according to a report from the Ministry of Economy and Finance (2013), and Morocco recorded an opening rate average in 2006–2011 equivalent to 60.5%, higher than in many emerging countries such as Egypt (39.5%), India (36.6%), Argentina (35.8%) and Turkey (43.6%). According to the International Chamber of Commerce Open Market Index (2015), Morocco and Saudi Arabia are considered the two most open countries in the MENA region.

This openness has encouraged the country's trade internationally, and particularly in exports, contributing to its economic growth. Between 2000 and 2011, the value of Moroccan exports grew at an annual average growth of 7.5%. This trend was maintained in 2015, with an annual growth beyond 7.1% improving the trade balance, especially with the imports decline of 6%.[11]

Similarly, the flows of FDI to Morocco reached US $2.16 billion in 2015, or 0.2% of the global FDI income and 6.8% of the total FDI to Africa (except for South Africa).[12] This is especially important when one considers that these FDI mainly concern the industrial sector, including the establishment of 200 international investors in the automotive sector and 100 in aeronautics.[13] They grew by 16.5% compared to 2014, which shows Morocco's attractiveness.

[11] http://www.huffpostmaghreb.com/2015/12/22/exportations-marocaines_n_8860946.html.

[12] http://www.economie.gouv.qc.ca.

[13] http://www.lavieeco.com/news/economie/les-details-de-la-nouvelle-strategie-industrielle-2014-2020-29129.html.

As part of the strategy of economic growth, SMEs and entrepreneurship play an important role, accounting for 95% of Moroccan enterprises. Their development should enable the country to increase international competitiveness and seize the opportunities of the local market. Thus, the state is committed to increase the productivity of SMEs and to promote the creation of new ones, especially through various funding programs (Imtiaz, Moussanada, etc.) and the establishment of four cities of SMEs based on business incubators. Such efforts place Morocco in the second position, after Qatar, where the density of new businesses is the largest in the MENA region, according to the 2016 Doing Business Report.[14]

The Role of Private Companies in Morocco

As part of the efforts deployed by the Moroccan government, private enterprises are essential to meet the socio-economic needs of the country. In general, they seek to generate growth in countries where unemployment is high and the influx of new job seekers is not easy to absorb. They also contribute to the creation of more wealth and the promotion of social inclusion. At an economic level, Moroccan private companies have increased employment opportunities by developing new products and exploring new markets. At a social level, and with a view to addressing the development challenges of the region, private companies should be ingenious when it comes to human development. They should promote sustainable development and social responsibility.

Private companies play an important role in the socio-economic development of Morocco by mobilizing along three axes: (1) Innovation and entrepreneurship; (2) Internationalization of markets; (3) Sustainable development and social responsibility.

In terms of innovation and entrepreneurship, Moroccan companies have shown sustained momentum in recent years. They have used their ability to innovate in order to create new needs in an increasingly modern society and to respond with solutions tailored to specific contexts. According to the World Bank (2013), the percentage of Moroccan firms

[14] Number of newly created businesses for every 1000 active persons aged between 15 and 64.

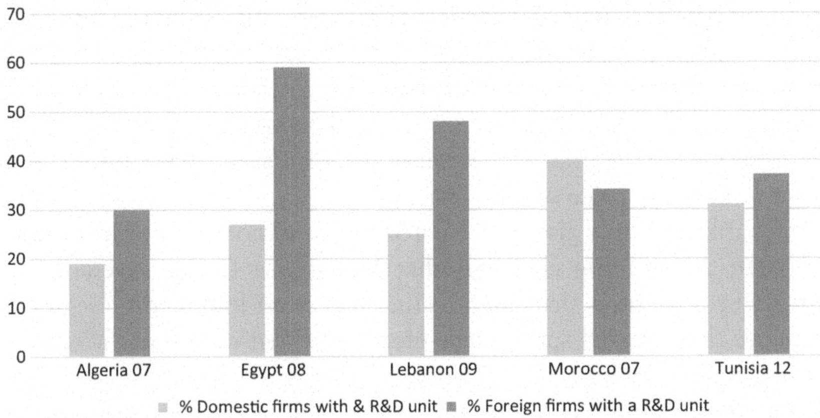

Fig. 7.8 The percentage of enterprises with R&D units in Morocco, according to their nature

that innovate is higher than that of multinationals operating in Morocco. This trend is confirmed by data from the World Bank (2016b) in terms of percentage of Moroccan exports with a high technology (6.6% in 2013 compared to 4.9 in Tunisia, 2.2 for Lebanon. 0.5 for Egypt, 0.7% for Saudi Arabia and 0.2% for Algeria). Moreover, the number of patent applications has doubled between 2011 and 2014. These efforts have allowed Morocco to rank 48th place in 2016 out of 200 in the ranking of Bloomberg's most innovative countries (Fig. 7.8).[15]

Moreover, between 2011 and 2014, the number of trademarks submitted by domestic companies grew by 12%. It has increased by 43.5% since 2006 to attain 6166 in 2014, compared to foreign brands that remain steady. The percentage of research and development (R&D) expenditures in terms of GDP in Morocco continues to be among the highest in the MENA region (World Bank 2016b). It should increase from 0.8% in 2013 to 1% in 2016 (Ministry of the Finance Economy 2015). As for patent applications with Moroccan origins, their number increased by 12% in 2014 compared to 2013 and doubled compared to 2010 (OMPIC 2014).

This dynamic innovation was the result of efforts deployed by several private enterprises. In the telecoms sector, companies have continued to

[15] http://www.bloomberg.com/graphics/2015-innovative-countries/.

introduce new products and services and to use original marketing techniques to attract more and more customers. In 2011, *Forbes Magazine* placed Morocco Telecom in 88th place in an index called Innovation Premium, just behind Microsoft.[16] This index measures how far innovation in terms of new products, services and/or markets has allowed companies to raise the price of their shares.

The banking sector also participated in the national innovation strategy. With the banking challenge that Morocco is facing, several banks have set up structures dedicated to the important low income segment. Therefore they created specialized subsidiaries that offer specific services to this segment. Indeed, the traditional banking sector was limited when it came to exploring this important area, namely because of agencies that were unsuitable, the offering of sophisticated banking deals compared to basic needs, and bankers who were poorly trained to serve these customers. The needs were simple, but banks have had to innovate strongly to satisfy them. This is the case of Wafacash, a branch of Attijariwafabank that after 15 years of activity in electronic banking and money transfer, has launched a single bank account, "Hissab Bikhir," which has simplified procedures. This banking solution has also been adopted by other Moroccan banks, such as Banque Populaire and Al Barid Bank, a subsidiary of the Moroccan Post Barid Al Maghrib. It is worth recalling that the banking sector is synonymous with financial inclusion and financial education, and consequently with development. Hence, the banking rate rose from 40% in 2008 to 64% in 2014 (Bank Al Maghrib 2014). These innovative offers accompanied different solutions that facilitate the collection and transfer of money at a local level. For example, these companies have managed to introduce a system of prepaid cards, which can be widely used and reinforce consumer confidence. This contributes to value creation for banks, but also has a significant impact on GDP growth.

Moroccan banks have also innovated by introducing mobile banking with Mobicash of Morocco Telecom, Pocket Bank or Banking Lilkoul of BMCE and Mobile Al Barid Bank, which since 2010 have allowed the

---

[16] http://www.marocnumericcluster.org/index.php?option=com_content&view=article&id=158%3Amaroc-telecom-parmi-les-100-entreprises-les-plus-innovantes-au-monde&catid=34%3Arevue-de-presse&Itemid=76&lang=fr.

transfer of foreign money to Morocco, bill payment and online shopping. These solutions have contributed to the financial inclusion of the previously unbanked Moroccan population. It is estimated that over half of phone users have access to financial services. Indeed, these services are open even to non-bank customers from the time they hold a mobile phone number.

In 2013, Al Barid Bank pushed this further by offering a cardless collection service on ATMs (automated teller machines: cashpoints), providing the opportunity for cash transfers and withdrawing cash without using a cash card. It also allows, also without a cash card, for agency or desk payable transfers, account-to-account transfers to a Barid Bank Mobile account or to a prepaid card, and other banking services. Thus, Al Barid Bank, a new entity created in 2010, now has 6 million customers, or one-third of unbanked people, and the number of accounts is increasing by 500,000 annually.[17] The bank has developed a partnership with the World Institute of Saving Banks and benefited from the development of IT (information technology) solutions dedicated to the electronic payment industry. In addition, it has forged partnerships with several departments and mobilized its wide network of 1870 branches in Morocco.

Similarly, consumer credit companies such as Wafasalaf have innovated in the field of risk analysis tools to take into account the informal nature of certain professions. For example, taxi drivers have been financed despite the unpredictability of their income and the lack of guarantees.

The revenue share of FDI in agri-food as a percentage of total FDI rose from 1.5% in 2010 to 26.2% in 2013. These results are based on the capacity of Moroccan companies to develop new products to satisfy the specific needs of society. In 2015, out of 11,709 trademark applications, the food industry was the most represented with 34%, and three categories in the top ten: plant food (16%), those of animal origins (10%) and unprocessed food (8%) (OMPIC 2014). These innovative efforts allowed the enhancement of local production through further processing processes and increasingly significant export dynamics (Fig. 7.9).

[17] http://www.lemag.ma/Une-Premiere-au-Maroc-Barid-Bank-lance-le-Mobile-Banking_a80894.html.

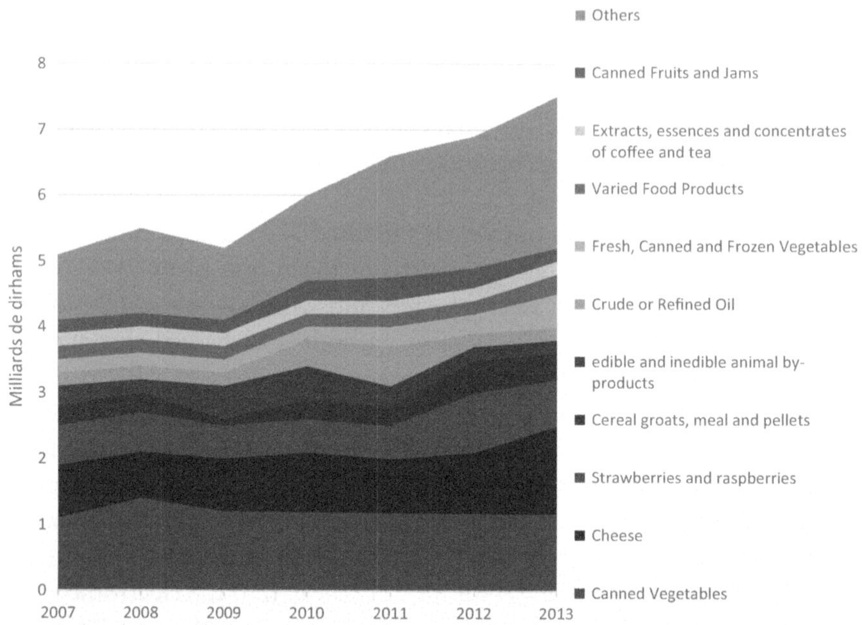

Fig. 7.9 The evolution of Moroccan exports of transformed agri-food products

Thus, from a market where only imported brands were available 20 years ago, we have moved to a market that is fiercely competitive and in which local brands are multiple and dominant in their respective segments. In just a few years, more products in the area of biscuits, chocolate, confectionery, jam, sauces, pasta, flour and so on have emerged. The buyback of foreign brands by Moroccan companies has also been noted, with companies developing products and making them even more successful. For example, the Moroccan group Unimer acquired the brand Pikamore from the French Amora, and is now one of the leaders in the sardine canning industry as well as in anchovies and frozen grilled marinated vegetables. It received the innovation award at the Agri-Food Industry Exhibition in France in 2014 for its brand Monégasque. In this way, the agricultural sector helped, through its investments, to improve the GDP growth rate to an average of 8.8% per year, according to the Ministry of Economy and Finance (2015).

Alongside the larger structures, SMEs have also followed this dynamic of innovation. It is worth mentioning that according to OMPIC (2014) 2014 was a record year in terms of the deposit of trade names for entrepreneurship, with 6000 more than in 2013, 66,770 in total. This increase depends on the development of the service (42%) and construction (31%) sectors. In terms of the actual number of created enterprises, it has increased by 4% compared to 2013, thanks in particular to the service sectors (35.1% as companies, 26.2% as individual businesses), trade (28.9% and 56.4%) and construction and real estate activities (24.2% and 6.8%).

In this sense, new technologies are increasingly important, thanks to the National Plan Morocco Numeric 2013 and the Morocco Plan. The most telling example is that of IT solutions in electronic banking, where HPS and M2M, along with other Moroccan companies, have managed to become regional and even worldwide players through their innovative capacity in a peak business (banking) and with a very demanding clientele. Besides, through the development of innovative solutions for electronic payment, M2M and HPS are selling their expertise, respectively to 350 financial institutions in 85 countries and 300 in 50 countries. Such a success is based on a strategic commitment in terms of HPS and M2M's innovation, with the companies respectively investing about 10.5% and 15% of their revenues in R&D, concentrated in Morocco. In 2014, HPS was able to increase its revenue by 10% and its consolidated net income by approximately 30%. For its part, M2M increased its consolidated results by 23%. To these two examples, we must add their colleagues, namely S2M and Finatech.

In this perspective, the aerospace and automotive sectors favored the technological development and enrichment of Moroccan production through sectors with higher added value such as wiring, mechanics, boiler making, composites, and mechanical assembling. Between 2008 and 2013, both sectors witnessed, respectively, an increase of 18% and 17.5% for exports and 16% and 14% in terms of highly qualified employment (Ministry of Economy and Finance 2015a). The sector has now increased to over 100 companies in just 12 years, and employs more than 11,000 young people. In 2014 it achieved a turnover of nearly US $1 billion, 4.5% of Morocco's exports compared to 1% in 2004, according to the Ministry of Economy and Finance (2015b). For their part, too, automotive companies have made a significant contribution to the Moroccan economy, in particular through the development of the cabling industry and car manufacturing. Exports marked a growth of 52.7% in 2014. At this level, international enterprises, notably the world leaders in the aeronautics sector, played a major role. To be mentioned are EADS, Boeing, Bombardier, Safran, Snecma, Creuzet/Indraero, Le Piston, Daher, Eaton, Aerolia and Alcoa, along with major players in the automotive industry such as Renault and Peugeot. It is also noteworthy that 2015 was a record year for the automotive industry in terms of export earnings.

Such efforts have transformed the structure of exports of Morocco in favor of technological areas, and have thus enhanced the competitiveness of the country. Automotive, aerospace, electronics and offshoring sectors have contributed to the increase in exports by all Morocco's global businesses by 86% between 2008 and 2013 (Ministry of Economy and Finance 2015b).[18] Consequently, the share of exports with a technological dimension has averaged 45.4% during the period 2009–2013, bringing the Moroccan economy closer to the world average of 56.7%. Fig. 7.10 compares the composition of Morocco's exports between 1998 and 2014.

In terms of market development, several Moroccan companies have explored new regions, especially in Africa. This internationalization has allowed Morocco to expand its external business transactions and therefore its revenues. Such international activity included, in 2014, 20 countries of sub-Saharan Africa, the first destination of Moroccan FDI in Africa, with 86% outbound to Africa and 50% of the total. This was an increase of 16% on average since 2003.[19] So, with about 480 strategic cooperation agreements, Morocco is the second largest African investor

[18] http://www.mcinet.gov.ma/ActualitesEvenements/Pages/Plan-d%E2%80%99acc%C3%A9l%C3%A9ration-Industrielle-2014-2020DOUBLEHYPHENl%E2%80%99a%C3%A9ronautique-se-dote-de-ses-premiers-%C3%A9cosyst%C3%A8mes.aspx.

[19] http://aujourdhui.ma/economie/relations-maroc-afrique-la-recette-miracle-de-boussaid-113343.

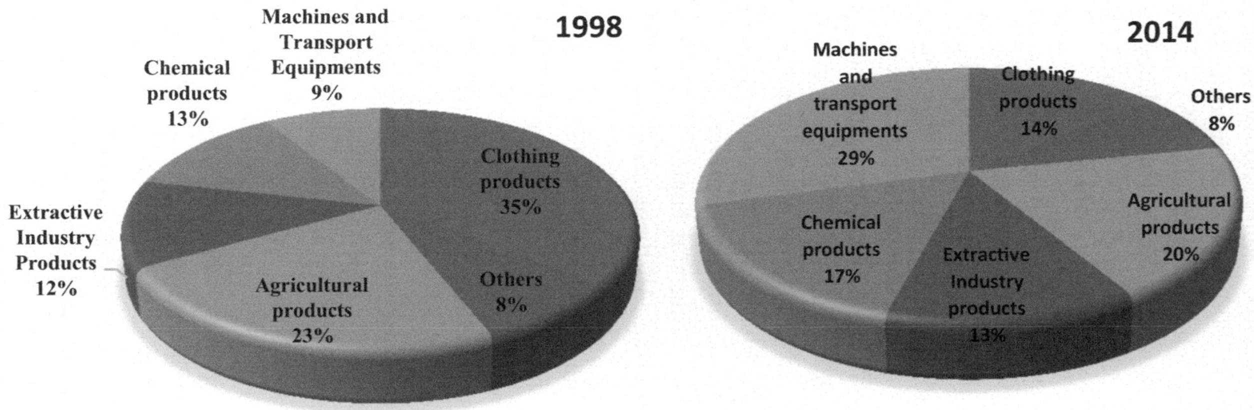

Fig. 7.10 The evolution of Morocco's exports structure between 1998 and 2004

in Africa. With respect to exports,[20] some 930 Moroccan exporting companies have signed about 12,000 contracts between 2009 and 2014. In 2010, Moroccan exports reached 7.2 billion DHS in 2010 (4.9% of total exports), three times the figure in 2000. Thus, Morocco's trade balance with sub-Saharan Africa went from a deficit of about 7.2 million DHS in 2000 to a surplus of US $2.7 billion in 2010.

There is no doubt that such a dynamic has been initiated and supported by the efforts of the Moroccan state at the economic level through public enterprises and at the political level through royal diplomacy; however, it relies increasingly on private companies. In this context, several companies are noteworthy: an airline company such as Royal Air Morocco, a Telecom operator such as Morocco Telecom, banks such as Attijari Wafa Bank and BMCE Bank of Africa or the Banque Centrale Populaire, an insurance company such as Saham, real estate operators such as Addoha, Alliances and Holmarcom, pharmaceutical companies such as Sothema, Parma 5 and Cooper Pharma, industrial players such as Ynna Holding and Schiele Morocco, consulting and engineering firms such as CID, Valyans or Capital Consulting. All these companies grew by exporting their expertise to Africa (Fig. 7.11).

Thus, 24% of the banking net product of Attijari Wafabank comes from its activities in North Africa and sub-Saharan Africa, with a growth rate that exceeds that of its national activities. In response to the immense banking needs expressed in Africa, Attijari Wafabank has successfully developed the largest network of branches (3331 at the end of 2014). Based on its national leadership, it pursues its expansion in Africa by transferring different sectors of expertise, starting with the transfer of money through its subsidiary Wafacash. The Moroccan bank has also developed in Europe to meet the needs of African residents abroad. For its part, Saham Group, especially in its insurance solutions, has developed a wide network of branches (over 650) in 20 African countries via 37 subsidiaries. The group intends to be the first insurance group in the continent outside South Africa.

In the construction sector, Addoha Group has been involved in real estate projects in over 16 African countries since 2011, and these are

---

[20] http://www.h24info.ma/economie/maroc/afrique-930-entreprises-marocaines-y-exportent-deja/21153.

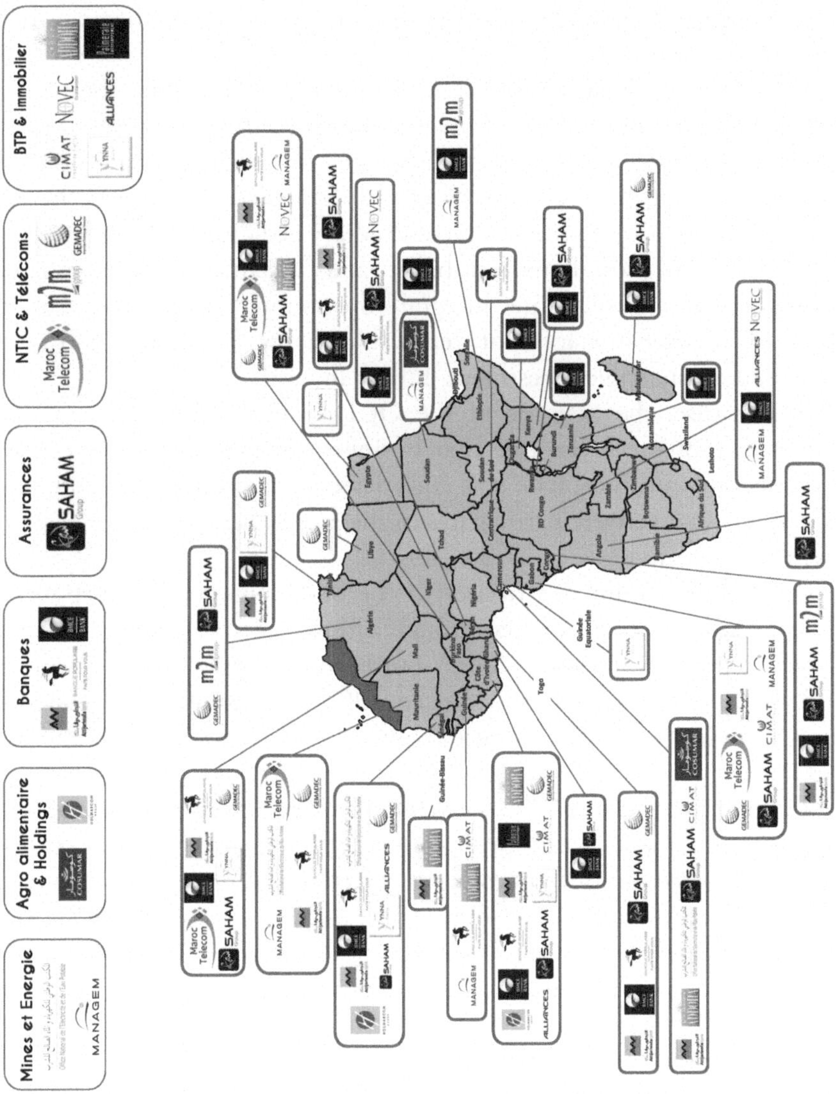

Fig. 7.11 Implantation of Moroccan companies at the African level

expected to generate US $2.2 million in revenue in 2016, selling one thousand apartments.[21] By 2018, Ciments Africa,[22] a subsidiary of

[21] http://www.leconomiste.com/article/921621-addoha-en-afriqueun-chiffre-d-affaires-s-curis-de-2-milliards-de-dh.

[22] http://lnt.ma/ciments-dafrique-et-addoha-un-duo-a-la-conquete-de-lafrique/.

Addoha, expects 20–25% of its revenues to be from sub-Saharan Africa through ten cement units.

The Moroccan pharmaceutical sector is also represented by companies at the international level. This involves not only exports carried out by several actors such as Sothema, Cooper Pharma, Pharma 5 and 36% of revenues coming from abroad,[23] but also Sothema's investment, in the first phase, of US$ 6.5 million in its subsidiary dedicated to West Africa.[24]

In terms of social responsibility and sustainable development, Moroccan private companies integrate the country's major concerns in the field of water management, renewable energy integration, and consistent and sustainable investment in human resources.

In this case, the example of the OCP Group is illustrative of the importance of the social role that business can play in the region. In 2014, Moroccan Phosphate was considered by McKinsey & Company as a model that actively participates in the economic and social development of the region.

First, OCP Group contributes to the development of its suppliers, subcontractors and customers through actions taken to strengthen their capacity and their technical skills.[25] Furthermore, being both a customer and the largest employer in Morocco, OCP Group not only generates direct employment opportunities, but also in terms of its economic partners.

The phosphate group is also actively involved in the educational sector. First, it created a non-profit organization, the Institute of Socio-Educational Promotion, to provide primary and secondary education to children from the areas of its operations. Second, it has invested in the creation of a polytechnic as part of a green city next to one of its mining sites, in order to contribute to the development of knowledge and good training skills. Third, it set up Skills Centers, which are local platforms for the development and promotion of the skills and talents of young residents and the children of retirees, providing learning programs,

---

[23] http://lematin.ma/journal/2015/pharma-5-met-le-cap-sur-l-afrique-anglophoneDOUBLEHYPHENet-l-europe-de-l-est/237466.html.

[24] http://www.medias24.com/ECONOMIE/ENTREPRISES/162-Sothema-vise-l-Afrique.html.

[25] http://www.ocpgroup.ma/.

staff development and promotion entrepreneurship. Finally, the OCP Group has offered for TPE and innovative entrepreneurs, capital access programs, participation in procurement and contracting, and technical assistance.

Finally, at the environmental level, OCP Group launched in 2009 the Green City Mohammed VI, an attractive and exemplary ecological living environment. The group also voluntarily adopted a strategy of sustainable development, meeting the needs of global agriculture, but also preserving the local environment and most particularly water resources. It was the first Moroccan company to join the program of Secure Management and Disposal of PCB (Polychlorinated Biphenyls), chemicals which are hazardous to health and the environment.

In the same spirit of social responsibility, the private sector will provide more opportunities for women to contribute to gender equity in the countries of the region. Their contribution through employability and entrepreneurship is an asset for the development of the region, but also helps to meet the expectations of millions of young people. For example, Morocco has legislated against discrimination in hiring women, but the culture and attitude in this context change slowly.[26] Other countries can undoubtedly follow, and several associations are working to promote women entrepreneurs and business leaders. The reality is that the number of women who are managing structured and significantly sized companies are very rare. The number of women who are directors of companies listed on stock markets in the Arab world is proof of this fact.

Accordingly, gender equity has been one of the axes that several private companies have focused on at the strategic level. For example, Wafasalaf made diversity one of the fundamental elements to ensure parity at both middle and top management levels. In fact, 51% of its workforce is composed of females. In parallel to its recruitment policy, the company organizes a series of conferences that are aimed at promoting gender equity and enhancing women's leadership.

[26] Morocco is the only country where it is prohibited by law to discriminate against women when giving them access to credit. Morocco and Djibouti are the only countries that legally mandate equal remuneration for equal work and non-discrimination based on gender in hiring for jobs.

In this spirit, and facing the problem of water scarcity in Morocco and especially its agricultural sector, Moroccan companies have committed to implement traditional or innovative ways in which to manage water efficiently. In the tourism sector, new hotels integrate treatment and water recycling systems and solar power generation. In February 2016 Morocco inaugurated the first phase of what is already the largest solar plant in the world, in the south of the country at Ouarzazate, Noor 1. This thermo-solar power plant produces 160 MW through the technology of cylindrical-parabolic sensors, and has a thermal storage capacity of three hours at full power. It allows thousands of households to access electricity on one hand and save 240,000 of CO_2 emissions per year on the other. The Moroccan plan for renewable energy is ambitious, aiming to achieve a 52% share of renewable sources in the energy mix by 2030, taking into account the growth in demand. This goal involves 20% from solar, 20% from wind and 12% from hydraulic systems.

The challenge that Morocco has to face is the development of new towns. It will have to integrate a range of solutions that promote sustainable development in these huge projects. This will include the management of water, electricity and sanitation, and also transport. The public companies that play the role of the state in these major projects must behave as experimental and implementational laboratories for solutions. Private companies will find added value through differentiation, such as by including solar water heating in social housing programs, thereby adding value for the target populations.

As part of their social and societal commitment, private companies in Morocco are actively supporting the educational sector. Indeed, private investors, through the opening of primary, secondary and tertiary schools, are expected to relieve the public sector, which cannot handle the significant flows of pupils and students and is subject to unprecedented overcrowding. They can therefore make a better offer that can meet the challenges of development not just in Morocco but also in other countries.

Moroccan private companies are also involved in the academic training process, assisting schools in developing appropriate programs in line with their needs. They encourage their managers to co-develop with schools training programs for their professions (MBA for Renault executives, Master in Insurance Management to support the strong growth in the sector, etc.), thereby opening their doors to research projects initiated by them and undertaking continuous educational activities.

Finally, Moroccan private companies support the educational system by providing training in business, with a view to promote the integration of young graduates. In this framework, HPS, among the top four global industries for electronic payment solutions for financial institutions, is a case in point. This Moroccan company set up an academy to allow its recruits from engineering schools and universities to acquire high-level technical skills. It was therefore able to focus on its Moroccan site, its IT solutions development activities addressing a demanding field, namely electronic banking, while developing local human resources.

In addition, the three telecoms companies have adopted a policy of social responsibility. According to its business and sustainable development report published in 2013,[27] in that year Morocco Telecom formalized its sustainable development policy, which revolves around three axes:

- The reduction of the digital divide and the dissemination of information technologies to isolated areas, as they contribute to improvements in living conditions and the enterprises' productivity. To that end, Morocco Telecom has invested in infrastructure and lower communication prices. This has allowed the company to serve 7200 towns between 2008 and 2013, with 97% access to the Telecommunications Access Programme (PACTE) and mobile Internet and multimedia services for 72% of Moroccans as opposed to 64.3% in 2012. Mobile communications prices were down by 27% in 2013, and those for fixed telephony by 11%, which resulted in an increase in mobile use of 15.6%;
- The support of employment: Morocco Telecom supports SMEs and professionals directly through appropriate technological solutions and indirectly through government programs that are dedicated to the promotion of information technology via awareness, initiation and reduced installation and subscription fees. In the same vein, Morocco Telecom has equipped and provided high-speed internet

[27] http://www.iam.ma/Lists/Tlchargement%20Finance/Attachments/535/Maroc-Telecom-rapport-d-activite-et-developpement-durable-2013.pdf.

access to the cooperatives of the solidarity-based economy and set up a virtual platform that connects them to Morocco Taswiq, a tool for the promotion of Moroccan products. Finally, Morocco Telecom has generated more than 127,000 indirect jobs in Morocco by giving 56% of its orders to local suppliers.

- The support of education: Morocco Telecom supports education by offering several scholarships through Morocco Telecom for business creation and promotion of jobs, created in 2006. In 2013 it also contributed to the dissemination of knowledge by granting about 50,000 students and over 178,000 teachers Internet connections and laptops at preferential prices, connecting 1300 schools to the Internet and equipping 390 multimedia rooms.
- The support of young athletes and artistic talents: Morocco Telecom supports several festivals (e.g. the Jawla Festival) and organizes tours through several villages in Morocco, along with competitions (e.g. the Mawazine Generation Contest) to allow Moroccan young artists to develop their talents. Morocco Telecom also supports athletes through partnerships with several federations and the creation or support of training centers, especially in football and athletics.
- Ethical management of its human resources and its relations with various economic players, as well as environmental protection: Morocco Telecom is actively involved in the training of its staff in these areas. In 2013, more than 3% of the payroll was dedicated to training programs. Since 2010, following its accession to the Global Compact of the United Nations, the company has integrated into its contracts Sustainable Development clauses, ensuring respect for human rights and labor law, and making commitments about the protection of the environment and the fight against corruption.

Ultimately, the development of enterprises in Morocco, as in other countries in the MENA region, commits these companies to fulfill their mission in their industry. It also engages them in social and human development. Expectations about the behavior of all parties are important, especially those of the younger generations in the city, country, region and global market.

Conclusion

This chapter has sought to understand how the private sector could contribute to the development of the MENA region. The region is facing significant socio-economic challenges. It must first generate sufficient growth in terms of GDP to mitigate the high unemployment rate which it suffers from, and particularly affects young people and women. Furthermore, the MENA region has witnessed major challenges in terms of the social inclusion of social services, gender equity, sustainable development and so on. Such challenges appear more urgent in the region in light of its young population, and also its tense geopolitical situation, owing to the armed conflicts raging in some countries and the political tensions prevailing in others.

In response to these challenges, the MENA region must focus more on the private sector. Indeed, the public sector is unable to guarantee high growth, especially with the oil crisis and the insecurity caused by terrorist groups that have resulted in decreasing public revenues and the disappearance of foreign investments.

In order to explore possible solutions that can enable the MENA region countries to promote the private sector, Morocco is an interesting case study. The country is experiencing sustained economic growth and a significant improvement in its human development levels. Morocco focuses, among other things, on private investment, both domestic and foreign. With this in mind, we are studying the way in which Morocco has promoted the creation and development of private enterprises while gradually putting in place an effective and transparent legal and administrative framework, facilitating access to finance and infrastructure (land, telecoms, etc.) and adopting an industrial emergence plan that promotes public/private partnerships and SMEs.

Consequently, we are interested in models and practices adopted by Moroccan private companies to support the socio-economic strategy of their country. At this level, three important areas are noteworthy: the development of new products and services; the internationalization of markets; and sustainable development and social responsibility. Thus, Moroccan private companies have succeeded in developing local consumption and expanding their markets, while taking into consideration the social issues of their country, especially the scarce water resources and social disparities.

That being said, this chapter should be followed by an empirical analysis that attempts to understand the obstacles that are still impeding the creation of business models and the dissemination of their practices. Indeed, the private sector in Morocco is growing, certainly, but above all this is thanks to larger enterprises. Hence, it is crucial to understand the dynamics needed to support SMEs and to integrate them into development, keeping in mind innovation, internationalization, sustainable development and corporate social responsibility. Finally, this analysis should involve other countries in the MENA region to enrich our thinking about the best solutions for promoting the private sector.

References

Bank Al Maghrib. (2014). *Rapport annuel sur la supervision bancaire*. Maroc.

European Bank for Reconstruction and Development. (2015). *Obstacles to business in Middle East and North Africa: Instability, corruption, informal sector*. London, United Kingdom.

FDI. (2014). *Foreign direct investment intelligence*. http://www.fdiintelligence.com/

IMF. (2015a). *Points saillants de la situation dans la région Moyen-Orient,* Afrique du Nord, Afghanistan et Pakistan (MOANAP). Washington, DC: USA.

IMF. (2015b). *IMF Country Report No. 15/43: Morocco*. Washington, DC: USA.

Institute for Economics and Peace. (2015). *Global Peace Index 2015: Measuring peace, its causes and its economic values*. New York, USA.

International Chamber of Commerce. (2015). *ICC open market index*. 3rd ed. Paris, France.

Loayza, N., & Wada, T. (2010). *Informal labor in the Middle East and North Africa: Basic measures and determinants*. Washington, DC: World Bank.

Ministry of Economy and Finance. (2013). *Compétitivité des exportations marocaines: Quel bilan?* Rabat, Maroc.

Ministry of Economy and Finance. (2015a). *Synthèse du Rapport Economique et Financier 2015*. Direction des Etudes et des Prévisions Financières. Ministère de l'Economie et des Finances. Maroc.

Ministry of Economy and Finance. (2015b). *Projet de loi des finances pour l'année 2016: Rapport économique et financier*. Ministère de l'Economie et des Finances. Maroc.

OECD. (2016). Retrieved from https://www.oecd.org/unitedstates/publicationsdocuments/reports/

Office Marocain de la Propriété Industrielle et Commerciale. (2014). Rapport d'activité 2014. Maroc.

Transparency International. (2015). *2015 Corruption perceptions index*. Berlin, Germany.

UNDP. (2014). *Rapport sur le développement humain: Pérénniser le progress humain*. New-York.

UNDP. (2015). *Rapport sur le développement humain: Le travail au service du développement humain*. New-York.

United Nations. (2007). *World poulation prospects: The 2006 revision*. New York, USA.

World Bank. (2008). *Note sur le secteur privé au Moyen-Orient et en Afrique du Nord*. Washington, DC.

World Bank. (2013). *Middle East and North Africa—Economic developments and prospects: Investing in turbulent times*. Vol. 1. Washington, DC.

World Bank. (2015). *Women, business and law 2016*. Washington, DC.

World Bank. (2016a). *Why MENA needs a new social contract*. Washington, DC. Consulté le 15 avril 2016.

World Bank. (2016b). *Base de données des indicateurs du développement mondial*. Washington, DC. Consulté le 15 avril 2016. http://data.worldbank.org

World Bank. (2016c). *Doing business 2016: Measuring regulatory quality and efficiency*. Washington, DC.

World Economic Forum. (2010). *The Middle East and North Africa at risk 2010*. Geneva.

World Economic Forum. (2015). *Global gender gap report*. Geneva.

WTO World Trade Organization. (1995). www.wto.org

8

Corporate Social Responsibility and Culture

Jacques Rojot

Introduction

In 1970, re-stating a point of view expressed more technically in 1962 in *Capitalism and Freedom*, Milton Friedman wrote in the *New York Times* for a general audience, expressing a point of view that was shared by many, that "The discussions of the 'social responsibilities of business' are notable for their analytical looseness and lack of rigor" and that businessmen declaiming "that business is not concerned 'merely' with profit but also with promoting desirable 'social' ends; that business has a 'social conscience' … [were] … preaching pure and unadulterated socialism" and were "unwitting puppets of the intellectual forces that have been undermining the basis of a free society these past decades."

According to this line of thought, the only social responsibility of business was and is to increase its profits. Employed by the shareholders,

J. Rojot (✉)
Université Paris II Panthéon-Assas, Paris, France

N. Azoury (ed.), *Business and Society in the Middle East*,
DOI 10.1007/978-3-319-48857-8_8

management was to be concerned only with profits, with, of course, due respect of the law and ethical custom.

The world has changed since 1970, and not only in terms of growth rate. We have moved from stockholder to stakeholder. Besides shareholders, new voices have appeared in order to take part in corporate governance. One can list non-exhaustively in addition to them: employees, clients, suppliers, customers, non-governmental organizations (NGOs), local communities, the general public, the environment and of course the State. Particularly noticeable in this respect is the green paper of the European Union (Commission of the European Communities 2001) promoting a European framework for corporate social responsibility. It considers, at European level, that corporate social responsibility includes human resource management, health and safety, adaptation to change, management of environmental impacts and natural resources, local communities, business partners, suppliers and consumers, human rights and global environmental concerns.

The Meaning of Social Responsibility for the Enterprise

From the academic point of view, corporate social responsibility has reached the status of a legitimate field of study, and an abundant stock of literature is ever increasing. More than ten years ago, it was argued that the field of corporate social responsibility "has grown significantly and today contains a great proliferation of theories, approaches and terminologies. Society and business, social issues management, corporate accountability are just some of the terms used to describe the phenomena related to corporate social responsibility in society. Recently, renewed interest for corporate social responsibilities and new alternative concepts have been proposed including corporate citizenship and corporate sustainability" (Garriga and Melé 2004).

Our purpose here is not to discuss the evolution of corporate social responsibility. This task is achieved in other chapters of this book. We simply want to underline an important issue and draw on its consequences when considering the issue of the generalized claim for the social responsibility of businesses.

Only a few years ago, one could have wondered if corporate social responsibility was not merely a new managerial fashion doomed to shortly disappear from our sight, as many others before, such as total quality, quality circles, re-engineering and the like. Some still wonder whether it is window dressing for management or a deep and real concern, but whatever the case is there is little doubt that there is a real and growing social demand, issuing from many quarters, for more socially responsible behavior on the part of business and corporations, ranging from ecologically responsible activity to ethical behavior. If it is a fashion, it seems to be a long-enduring one. One might still agree with Milton Friedman, but, even if that were to be the case, business has taken note of corporate social responsibility and begun to take it into account, as the multiplicity of codes of behavior, international norms and the like witness.

However, what we would like to underline first is that there is a major conceptual dividing line. Two different understandings of the meaning of corporate social responsibility are possible.

According to an EU green paper (Commission of the European Communities 2001), "Most definitions of corporate social responsibility describe it as a concept whereby companies integrate social and environmental concerns in their business operations and in their interaction with their stakeholders on a voluntary basis. Being socially responsible means not only fulfilling legal expectations, but also going beyond compliance and investing 'more' into human capital, the environment and the relations with stakeholders." Thus, to its stakeholders, a business adds to financial responsibility commercial, social and environmental ones.

Even then, two concepts of corporate social responsibility are possible, and they overlap only partly, if at all. On the one hand, it is a case of acknowledging that a new multiform social demand is emerging around corporate social responsibility. Thus business must answer that demand. However, in order to face the additional turbulence in the environment, new tools and mechanisms must be adopted, roughly similar to the ones traditionally adapted to environmental changes for business. It is necessary to adapt to new external constraints, even if they are different from those that existed in the past. Enterprises will then try to design, together with the new stakeholders, new rules of the game. On the other hand, corporate responsibility might be considered as an internal constraint.

The ever-adapting capitalistic model is evolving again and must integrate these new aspirations. Business must become conscious of the need to manage differently. Notably, ethics must become an essential component of management.

In both cases, of course, management must be concerned, but not in the same way. If corporate social responsibility is conceived within the first concept, what is mostly needed is the addition of new tools to the manager's standard equipment. These could include global compliance programs, ethical investments, recognized norms, codes of conduct, corporate or international, ethical investment funds, social rating agencies ratings, partnerships with NGOs, and integration of programs and objectives related to sustainable development. The adoption and use of these tools by the manager will be enough in his eyes to discharge the new social responsibility that society has placed over business. They will play the same role as the managerial actions geared to avoid harassment that are promoted by sentencing guidelines in the USA. Management can then consider that it need not be concerned by further issues.

If corporate social responsibility is conceived within the framework of the second concept, we are looking at a totally different case. The issue is now to try to integrate in depth an ethical dimension to the expectations, attitudes and behaviors not only of management but also of employees at all levels of responsibility. Thus employees must subscribe to the new way of doing business. Managerial and employee behavior must move towards a concern for equity. It is no longer a matter to act within the letter of the new rules, but according to a deep feeling that what one is doing is right, according to principles that are considered to be equitable, and not simply following the letter of the law. The first concept remains within well-defined legal ground, the second moves into a moral area.

Two other dimensions must then be distinguished for each concept: an internal and an external aspect. Internal concerns the relationship between top management and the employees, and external concerns the relationship between the enterprise and its environment. The latter requires the company to demand and secure ethical behavior of all its employees in regard to all other stakeholders.

The first approach seems unavoidable, given the extent of social demands, but is probably insufficient. It can be summarized by the conclusions of the trend towards "business ethics." However, can one be sure that "ethics pays"? Is the rather restrictive understanding of ethics being limited to following the rules in itself a factor of business success? It might be true in the long term, through building a climate of trust around the enterprise concerned. But the pressure of the short term in a very competitive world might well compromise the long-term perspective. As the world is moving quickly, and is partly if not largely practicing various degrees of corruption, there will be very strong incentives to adopt practices that are common within the industry and/or the country of operation, notwithstanding internal rules and regulation.

Besides, this approach is not entirely practical, except in the simplest cases where it is easy to decide if an established rule has been broken or not. Usually this is not the case, as rules have limits in applicability which are reached very quickly when one moves on to more complex ground. Yet most of the questions and issues involving corporate social responsibility are not simply problems, or even complex problems, but dilemmas with contradictory and paradoxical aspects. In these cases, a rule that is intended to guide decision and action is of little help in starkly different contexts. Depending on the place, the time and the circumstances of the decision and action, the ethical and socially responsible answer may well be different from the conventional answer, and/or pose a dilemma that it is difficult to solve. For instance, should one make redundant a group of employees, including some who are over 50 years of age, condemning them to virtually indefinite unemployment in the present market conditions, and perhaps to poverty until they reach retirement age, or should one keep them on the company payroll and risk compromising the future of a small business, with the potential conclusion being bankruptcy and unemployment for all the employees? Should companies continue to externalize the cost of recruitment to the educational system, thereby sentencing whole categories of youth to exclusion from the labor market? It is certainly wrong to steal, but could not a labor court in a developing country decide that, in order to justify dismissal, a theft by an employee should be of such extreme seriousness and occur within such extreme circumstances as to be liable for the death penalty? The grounds for the decision could be that death, in the local conditions of employment, was the quasi-unavoidable result of unemployment after dismissal (Rojot 1994).

The two conceptions of corporate social responsibility must thus be combined. The first alone is insufficient. Taking for granted the inclusion of new regulating tools into the manager's standard equipment, how is it possible to move forward?

A first consideration is that, to some extent, the two conceptions are compatible at an elementary level. It is indeed true that, to a limited but real extent, discharging its social responsibilities can be a useful management tool for a company. This is the case in at least three aspects: coordination, attracting talent and keeping talented employees.

As far as the first aspect is considered, the process of managerial training for higher positions could be made easier by learning socially responsible behavior. The line of reasoning is the following: enterprises, at least large ones, must reconcile their needs for decentralization and coordination. This is to some extent a concept at the heart of organization theory (Mintzberg 1979). In principle it applies to all organizations, but the large multinationals were the first to feel it most acutely in practical terms. They were torn between two contradictory imperatives: on the one hand the demands of host countries, notably in terms of local recruitment, not only for manpower but also local management, even top management; and on the other hand the need to use the competitive advantage of a unique center for decision-making that was located in the home country. This problem has spread to all large multiple-unit enterprises as they face a more turbulent environment and an increased demand for flexibility and different modes of organization in their business units. The solution, for potential management, is arrived at through a journey of specially selected job postings at different levels of responsibilities within differently located subsidiaries and/or units. Through this, a trainee can learn from the example of superiors and colleagues when confronted by hard decisions, learning how to practically implement a set of abstract principles and values in order to conform to corporate policy. More than a set of concrete and precise rules, subject to the drawbacks underlined above, this learning process across drastically divergent environments and circumstances is conducive to a sophisticated way of dealing with dilemmas within corporate guidelines. At the end of the process, the trainee will be able, when in a position of responsibility, to apply a decision-making process guided by lived examples that conforms to corporate policies.

It is within these policies that socially responsible behavior should be integrated.

Taking the second aspect of corporate responsibility into account, the recruitment of talented young future managers, which is a critical issue for all businesses, can also be a major asset.

The younger generations of educated managerial employees are sensitive to various aspects of social responsibility, particularly but not only concerning ecology and environment, when deciding which enterprise to join in a labor market that is always competing intensely for talent. For instance, an interesting study carried out in 2002 in France, on a sample of more than 600 relevant individuals, indicated that two of the three most important aspects of their work for young managerial employers were the usefulness of the work performed for society (82% of the sample) and the values of the enterprise within which they were working (76% of the sample.) (Institut de l'Entreprise 2002). These elements were also among the three most important in selecting a job.

It is one thing for an enterprise to recruit talented young managerial employees; it is another one to keep them. The same study evidenced a set of findings concerning the relationship felt by the same young managerial employees towards the enterprise that was employing them. As foreseen, the study made it clear that the old reciprocal commitment between the (French) manager and his enterprise, exchanging absolute loyalty for lifetime employment, was no longer viable. This was to be expected in a generation that was aware of downsizing and the restructuring of enterprises, and also the experience of unemployment, by a family member or close relative if not directly. This constitutes the endpoint of a movement that started quite some time ago and was noticed with foresight by Crozier (Crozier 1978). However, neither do the younger generations hold a mercenary view of employment, where job-hopping takes place at the slightest monetary incentive. The old unwritten but enforced deal has been replaced by an implicit psychological contract (Coyle-Shapiro and Parzefall 2008), clear and readable, bilateral, at the level of reciprocal expectations, operating in the short term, where not only material but also immaterial elements are included. Prominent among the latter are the values of the enterprise that employs the young manager. The understanding of these values was wide, including not only those publicly posted by top management, but also (and mainly) the way in which they were daily presented and lived in the day-to-day operation of the business. Thus, enforcement of its social responsibilities by the employing enterprise constitutes a powerful tool for enhancing the commitment of the managerial employee to the company.

However, beyond the basic level constituted by the three considerations outlined above, corporate social responsibility in the second understanding outlined below requires deeper changes if an ethical and socially responsible dimension is going to be integrated in the expectations, attitudes and behaviors not only of top management and management but also of all employees at all levels of responsibility, internally and externally.

Doing this requires much deeper changes in the ways of doing business. It requires in fact a change in culture. However, this is easier said, or written, than done.

Culture

The first step, and the one to which we must limit ourselves here, is to understand what culture is and what it means.

The word culture is difficult to define precisely since it has different meanings in different domains of social science. Morin (2001) lists five of them: two refer to anthropology. In the first, culture is opposed to nature, and includes everything which does not refer to the innate traits of the individual. In the second, it applies to everything which has meaning; in other words, all human activities. Another meaning belongs to ethnography, where culture is opposed to technology and includes beliefs, values, rites, norms and patterns of behavior. Another, from the domain of sociology, includes the area of affects, of the personality, of sensitivity and social links. Finally, in a literary context culture refers to classical humanities and to literary and artistic taste. In behavioral science, the most often used definition refers to the pattern of beliefs, values and modes of communication and cognition that influence how human senses perceive and react to stimuli, which is Morin's third category. In other words (Goldman and Rojot 2003), culture provides the distinctive manner in which we imagine reality.

Culture has also been evoked in the literature at at least three levels: national, occupational and organizational. We have noted elsewhere (Rojot 2008; Chanut and Rojot 2009) that the concept of national culture raises several issues, generally speaking, for management and organization theory, but also for our understanding of corporate social responsibility if we hope that culture can be modified in order to integrate the second of the concepts outlined above.

If we look first at national culture, it has been intuitively felt for a long time that culture influences nations, and that there is something which could evoke the idea of a national culture. Montesquieu developed a theory of the impact of climates on mankind and Pascal wrote that "Vérité en-deça des Pyrénnées, erreur au-delà" (What is held true this side of the Pyrenees is held wrong on the other), underlying the differences between two national cultures.

More recently than the philosophers of a bygone era, several observers have noted the influence of national culture on organizations and on various aspects of management. The surge of a new wave of interest in this can probably be dated to Hall's work (Hall 1959, 1969, 1976). He identified two major conceptual dimensions of culture. On the one hand, high context and low context cultures differ through the amount of implicit pre-programmed information that is vested in the communication act against the explicit information contained in the message. On the other hand, cultures differ in the way they regard the impact of time. Monochronic cultures have a rigid conception of time, focusing on one thing at a time and separating interpersonal relations from scheduled work activities. Conversely, polychromic cultures have a flexible and fluid conception of time, conduct multiple varied activities together and allow interpersonal relations to interfere with scheduled work activities.

Kluckholn and Strodtbeck (1961) identified six dimensions in which cultures differ: relationship to nature, human relationships, truth and reality, human nature, human activity and attitudes towards time and change.

Hofstede (1980, 1991) has probably done one of the most extensive experimental studies based on international survey research in a multinational corporation. He defines culture as the "collective mental programming of people in an environment." At a national level these cultures differ in four respects : (1) Power distance, which is the degree of social acceptance of the unequal distribution of power in organizations and institutions. (2) Uncertainty avoidance, which is the degree to which a society tries to avoid ambiguous and uncertain situations which it perceives as threatening. Consequently, it provides greater stability, more formal rules, is less tolerant of deviant ideas and behaviors, and believes in the attainability of absolute truths and expertise. It is correlated with a higher degree of anxiety and aggressiveness, of which one of the by-products is a strong inner urge to work hard. (3) A continuum of individualism–collectivism, going from a relatively loosely knit framework of social relations where people take care of themselves towards a network of tight groups where people look after each other and to which they owe absolute loyalty. (4) A continuum from "masculinity" to "femininity" in the dominant social values, in other words encompassing the values on which, in all societies in the sample, men scored relatively higher than women in a positive sense, whatever the global score for the society itself, with gender roles clearly distinguished. Masculinity includes assertiveness, the acquisition of money and things, not caring for others, not caring for quality of life, not caring for people. A fifth dimension was added later that deals with long-term against short-term orientation.

Continuing the same line of research Trompenaars and Hampden Turner (1997), basing their findings on samples of managers from different companies, identify seven value orientations along seven continua: universalism versus particularism (general application of rules as opposed to personalized relationships), individualism versus communitarianism (acting as an free isolated individual as opposed to acting as a member of a community), neutral versus emotional (objective, dispassionate as opposed to subjectively demonstrating emotions) diffuse versus specific (involvement with others in all dimensions of working as well as private life as opposed to segmentation into discrete and unrelated parts), achievement versus ascription (social status gained by achievements as opposed to social status resulting from position in social hierarchies), human–time relationship (sequential organization of time with punctuality as opposed to synchronic multitask performance with reorganization of time being a function of circumstances), and human–nature relationship (trying to control the environment as opposed to adapting to it).

Schneider (1985) reviews the literature around the categories defined by Hofstede and by Kluckholn and Strodbeck. These are relationship to nature, human relationship, truth and reality, human nature, human activity, and attitudes towards time and change. She finds a that French national culture has a significant impact on strategy formulation by enterprises. It is characterized along the following dimensions: passive instead of active monitoring of environment; preference for qualitative instead of quantitative information; preference for sources of information that are more subjective and personal, or emanating from authorities; preference for a logical analytical approach rather than mathematical decision models; different sets of priorities that will be developed in terms of importance, urgency and certainty; and a focus that will be internal rather than external.

Maurice et al. (1982), studying similar enterprises in the same industries in France and Germany, noted intriguing differences. The average wage for a blue-collar worker compared to that of a white-collar employee was lower in France than in Germany. White-collar employees were not only better paid but also proportionally more numerous in France. 40% only of French workers, against 75% in Germany, were holders of a vocational degree. German foremen were also less numerous than the French. The differences were explained by the role of continuing education in Germany, based on the system of training between school and plant for "meisters". This system allows workers, throughout their professional life, to accumulate degrees up to the level of graduate engineer. This scale of degrees is a condition for promotion, whereas in France promotion is granted more as a function of the seniority and "potential" of the individual, or his initial training. The French training system is narrowly related to mobility and firm-specific skills, whereas the German system, with lifelong vocational training, gives access to nationally recognized degrees. It allows interenterprise mobility at various levels of technical job ladders. Conversely in France, because the training is enterprise-specific, interenterprise mobility is hampered. Promotion is therefore dependent more on change of status than on moves on a technical ladder. The German foreman, holder of a technical degree, enjoys more autonomy and prestige than his French equivalent. In turn, both training and mobility are related to organizational features, with a larger span of control for foremen and more multiskilling for workers in Germany.

Rojot (1988) has attempted to explain the differences in nature and structure between collective agreements in the USA and in France by the national cultural traits that permeate the legal systems of the two countries. He notes that the differences in the regulation of collective agreements can be explained by the primacy of the individual contract of employment over the collective agreement, the duty to perform being replaced by a duty to pay damages, and the presence of a minimal extended floor of statutory protection in the case of France. Those explanatory factors can be traced back to cultural values. In France the absolute primacy of the formal rights of the individual reigns supreme, and the only allowable limits can issue from a generally applicable public policy that is embodied in imperative, substantial and normative compulsory provisions for the equal good of all citizens, issued by a dirigist and interventionist central government.

Trepo (1975) attributes the failure of efforts to introduce management by objectives in France to the fear of face-to-face conflict, the way in which authority is conceived and the mode of selection of top managers. He demonstrates that subordinate managers, even though they may formally and vocally want more responsibility, actually remain passive, looking mostly for protection from above and avoiding commitment to specific objectives. Reciprocally, top managers, who rule autocratically, see the company as a kind of elite school, where to be the boss means to be the most intelligent one, and therefore they consider that subordinates cannot conceivably have valid ideas to offer. Of course, this does not mean that management by objectives or evaluation of performance according to a similar system is not practiced in France; far from it. However, in many cases, the system of management by objectives as it is applied in practice in companies is only remotely linked to the objectives assigned to it by its original promoters and takes a wholly different meaning, even if its form is apparently respected.

However, the national level is not the only one at which culture operates. It should be considered at least under two other aspects that make the matter more complex. On the one hand, other researchers, in limited numbers, in parallel and separately, sometimes with a different perspective and scientific agenda, have focused their work upon the concept of occupational cultures, cutting across both national and organizational cultures. Common bonds of occupation or avocation give rise to a group with the same culture that uses its own specialized vocabulary, assumptions, formats and traditions for internal communication. Such groups sometimes also share values and goals respecting their common endeavor that may, to a degree, cut across cultural as well as sub-cultural groupings. Among the more limited scholarly analysis along those lines, two sources must be quoted. Sainsaulieu (1977, 1982) derives from empirical studies the conclusion that employees at work build rules, values and practices, which are elaborated in common to manage their reciprocal relationships such as solidarity, mutual help, technical complementarity, dependence, authority, on the job training, information, control and appraisal. In that way a kind of community is built around what constitutes an occupational or trade culture, such as is the case for instance for metalworkers, sailors, miners and railway workers. This community is significant in the day-to-day running of organizations and also in labor conflicts. This is the case at national level as much as at enterprise level, which demonstrates that such occupational cultures cut across organizations. More generally, an in-depth study of workers in industry demonstrates four types of culture among the working class during the 1960s period of economic growth, confirmed by later studies: fusion, for unskilled labor, negotiation for highly skilled blue-collar employees and technical staff, affinity for self-made supervisory staff and withdrawal for minorities.

With the purpose of introducing the methods of ethnology into organizational culture studies, Gregory (1983), who defines culture as "learned ways of coping with experience," has studied professionals working in Silicon Valley enterprises. She reaches similar conclusions, putting forward evidence of "occupational communities" around different cultures, which are not simply sub-cultures but cross-cut organizational lines and provide employees with significant reference groups outside as well as inside a company. Such are, for instance, the cultures of computer scientist, software engineer and marketer.

However, a new and different concept of culture has come to cut across the previous ones at another level. This was no longer aimed at national or occupational level, but at the organizational one. The focus of attention was no longer the country or the occupation but the organization, and often specifically the enterprise. Culture was for instance seen as the factor that unifies and unites an organization through its management by leaders (Schein 1985). This perspective asserts that managers can control organizational culture and even make it their most important tool. Accordingly, a strong culture is healthy for an organization; everyone should share this culture and use it to guide decision-making. Along those lines, Johnson (1988) proposed the notion of the "cultural web" of an organization, from which emerges the dominant paradigm which constrains its strategic choices. The paradigm is "the set of beliefs and assumptions held relatively common through the organization, taken for granted, and discernible in the stories and explanations of managers, which plays a central role in the interpretation of environmental stimuli and configuration of organizationally relevant strategic responses." This is a definition close to the one given by Schein for corporate culture.

This emerging paradigm is in turn maintained and activated by a stable and reinforcing cultural web in the organization that contains not only myths, rituals, symbols, control systems and power structures, both formal and informal, but also organizational and technical structures, and processes and routines that implicitly embody them, through taken-for-granted assumptions in the way of that operational daily business is conducted.

The elements of this web are mutually reinforcing : for instance, the power structure has a vested advantage in maintaining things as they are and manages the control systems to silence or expel dissenters, while celebrating rituals which demonstrate the legitimacy of its own power (senior partners bringing in critical business in a law firm against other partners, junior members, paralegals, secretaries or engineers in an aerospace firm only being granted access to top management). At the same time, the way of doing business privileges, for instance, technological choices over marketing or financial ones. The location of operations follows technical imperatives in terms of supplier availability and/or easy contact with fellow engineers from other firms.

The notion of organizational culture as a useful tool of management introduced a lively debate and was widely criticized in many quarters. It also introduced a volume of literature that is too important to be simply summarized here. An early account of the controversy is, for instance, offered by Lynn Meek (Meek 1988). For instance, one statement nicely points out a major criticism of the view of culture as management tool: "culture is something an organization is, not something that an organization has" (Smircich 1983); thus it is not susceptible to managerial manipulation.

Culture and Bounded (Limited) Rationality

There are, however, problems with the concept of culture, at whatever level it is considered, national, occupational or organizational. On the one hand, there are often different groups within a culture. Important variations from a culture's characteristic behavioral norms reflect differences in the identity of religious, linguistic, ancestral or regional groups, among other variables. These differences resulting from identity groupings may often be referred to as sub-cultures. But, where do the borders of a sub-culture start, since no culture or sub-culture is homogeneous? Any given cultural trait, say tolerance to hierarchy, for any given cultural group must be considered as an average, a mean for that group. However, around that mean, individuals may show wide variations, and the standard deviation on that given characteristic may be important, even very important. Thus, one may find oneself, within a culture generally rated low on hierarchical distance, in front of an individual who personally sits three standard deviations from the mean and happens to give a huge importance to that characteristic.

Several other potential problems can be identified. The first is that whenever an observer takes note of a cultural characteristic, the accuracy of that observation must be discounted by recognizing that it is a product of the observer's own cultural orientation (Lederach 1995). In other words, observations about a given culture from the part of a stranger tell us as much if not more about the culture of that stranger that about the culture he observes. The deepest influences emanating from culture consist of assumptions that are so well embodied in us that they are "taken for granted" without being identified as cultural traits. For most Europeans, the British do not drive on the left of the road, they drive "on the wrong side" (Schneider and Barsoux 1997). Secondly, cultural differences are not absolutes; they are matters of degree. For example, no culture is wholly "communal" or "individualistic" in its value orientation. In addition, what we call "culture" is the composite of a group's normative characteristics. However, no one person can be expected to fully personify a given culture. Each individual's personality is a unique variation from the cultural norm and, from the perspective of its norms, as underlined above, some members of a cultural group may be quite "abnormal." Moreover, although cultural norms have a substantial impact on behavior, "individuals can and do act apart from cultural demands" (Adler and Jelinek 1994).

Another major issue is that culture changes over time. However, from a theoretical point of view, the notion of change in culture poses several problems. If the culture is our beliefs, values, modes of communication and cognition, then it conditions our view of the world, not the other way around. Thus it cannot willingly be changed and its change requires a puzzling theoretical explanation. This issue deeply questions "cultural engineering" and/or managing organizational cultures. Top management *is* part of the culture of a company, thus how can it change it willfully and voluntarily? This does not mean that top management does not influence it, on the contrary, but much of this influence on one hand is not consciously conducted and on the other hand is mediated by others who are involved in the organization.

At another level, the idea of national culture indicates that we need an answer to the question of change. When, and how, does national culture change? A theory of culture unable to answer that question loses much of its explanatory usefulness. If it is rigid, if national traits are impervious to change, it runs into the face of experimental evidence. European and American societies have undergone deep changes in recent years over little time, for instance regarding the death penalty in criminal cases or the status of same sex marriage. If, on the contrary, cultural traits become so flexible that they can be molded by any fashion arising, the concept is no longer useful. A permanently changing culture simply reproduces the changes in the environment around itself. What then is significant?

In addition, a question is then raised about the harmonization of occupational or corporate culture and national culture. Which one dominates the other, for instance within a multinational corporation? And under what conditions does this happen? Do they merge (and if so into what?) or produce organizational conflict?

In our view, a way to solve these multiple problems would be to adopt a different view of culture. We have proposed elsewhere (Rojot 2008; Chanut and Rojot 2009) that we should consider culture as sets of shared limitations on rationality.

The concept of culture becomes much more useful if we interpret it in such a way. This interpretation addresses some of the issues that other cultural theories ignore.

The concept of bounded rationality is well known. It has been elaborated and proposed by Simon (1947), expanded upon by Boudon (1976) and by Crozier (1963) and Crozier and Freiberg (1977), and is often used. Simply put, the limits of rationality derive from the inability of the human mind to make a single decision on all the aspects of value, knowledge and behavior that would be relevant.

However, this should not be construed as meaning that individuals are going to act randomly or irrationally. Within the framework of their limited knowledge, capacities and means of action, they are going to try to select a preferred alternative. Therefore they are not irrational, but rather their rationality is limited; it is bounded. That is to say, in practice individuals cannot be considered as totally rational, but not because they follow a line of behavior which is irrational. On the contrary, their behavior is almost always rational, for them. But it is not objectively and totally so if seen by an outside observer, because they act within a framework bounded by their limited capacities and are facing too rich and too complex a world.

This framework is bounded in two dimensions. On the one hand, perfect rationality would drive us to assume a synoptic and maximizing attitude. It is synoptic in the sense that all costs and benefits would be weighed, that all possible alternative courses of action would be considered together, and maximizing in the sense that they could be considered in all their potential consequences, and that the one course of action maximizing the satisfaction and minimizing the dissatisfaction of the individual concerned would be selected. All costs and benefits incurred would be considered by him. We know that this cannot be the case, for there is not enough time or information to register, and even less to consider, all likely courses of action, and the human mind is too limited to analyze them, were they to be available. Additionally, the world is too uncertain and turbulent to allow one to assess all the potential consequences of a course of action with any degree of foresight. Thus, instead of being synoptic, the consideration of alternatives is sequential and, instead of maximizing, the selection of one is only satisfying.

On the other hand, the limits to rationality also play at a second level, and a more complex one. It is the one that Simon (1947) calls the internal environment of the decision-maker, his ability to build and represent for himself the outside world. The environment is no longer given and more or less well perceived by the decision-maker, it is to be constructed actively by him. There is no longer only objective outside data, ignored or more or less accurately represented, but also subjective input built into the decision-making process. Situation and process interact.

Limitations on rationality form a continuum with an increasing degree of complexity that includes nationality, occupation and organization. The simplest limitations on rationality may be the physical and biological ones. Psychology has demonstrated that perception takes place through the simultaneous operation of selection, structuration and interpretation (Hirst 1965). Hence, even at the most basic levels, different individuals perceive different realities. When an individual interacts with others in situations that are more complex, additional limitations on rationality come into action. In a way, the next basic level of limitations is made up of rules (national laws, occupational customs, organizational regulations). These rules place very visible and obvious limitations on the rationality of members of collectivities. Whether they obey the rules or not is irrelevant because they influence behavior, even when individuals seek to escape their influence or to circumvent them. In addition, people in collectivities build shared stocks of knowledge and they construct reality by typifying habitual actions (Berger and Luckmann 1966). These shared typifications mean that members of a group share views of reality and develop accepted ways to do things. These typifications influence not so much the process of decisions as their premises.

Conclusion

Within this understanding, the concept of culture becomes at the same time clearer and conceptually useful. At the various levels considered, shared limits on rationality influence and frame behavior and the understanding of situations. The cultural change implied in taking corporate social responsibility seriously requires that the premises of the thinking of the individuals concerned change. Following that, behavior and decision-making will change. How is that to be implemented? Changes in law, corporate charters and regulations are necessary but insufficient. They will have to be reinforced and complemented by the collective sharing of a new way of shaping reality at international, national and organizational levels. This can only be built from the bottom, day to day, through visible and multiple examples of pragmatic, operational priority being given to corporate social responsibility at all levels of organizations in day-to-day business. Differences will come from the way in which any given individual immersed in a national, occupational, organizational environment will accommodate in his accepted behavior and cognitive limits a new set of limits on his rationality alongside the other sets of limits already present that come from other sources drawn from his personal experience. The changes in culture, in turn, occur when enough individuals share a limit of some sort. It requires a recourse to Giddens to explain the mechanics: the reproduction of accepted and shared ways of behavior and cognition in day-to-day interactions between individuals. The characteristics of duality and recursivity evidenced by Giddens (1976) explain how individuals create and reproduce limits on their rationality. Social activities are influenced by limits which are not created ab initio by individuals but ceaselessly recreated by them, through the use of the very means which allow them to express themselves as actors, the limits themselves upon which they draw. Conditions allow the social activities of individuals and by their activities, the individuals create and reproduce the very conditions which make these activities possible. Giddens (1984) uses the example of language to illustrate the point: language allows individuals to communicate, and by communicating they produce and keep alive the language. Cultural change becomes even more complex this way: it is neither voluntary nor directed, but a common result of interactions in varying conditions. Reproduction is also production, in that it contains potential germs of change, consequences of reflexivity in a contextualized environment, unexpected effects and unrecognized conditions from action. At any given moment individuals share in various amounts of a cognitive limit from total absence to full influence. When enough of them, after interactions in context, partake of it, it becomes a more generalized limit on cognition; in other words, the equivalent of a cultural trait. It is the only way through which corporate social responsibility may become a serious new way of doing business.

Bibliography

Adler, N., & Jelinek, M. (1994). Is organization culture culture bound. In G. Weaver (Ed.), *Culture and conflict: Readings in intercultural relations, University Press of Mississippi, USA*.

Berger, P. L., & Luckmann, T. (1966). *The social construction of reality*. New York: Doubleday.

Boudon, R. (1976). *La logique du social*. Paris: Hachette.

Chanut, V., & Rojot, J. (2009). Culture et organisation. In J. Rojot, P. Roussel, & C. Vanderberghe (Eds.), *Comportement organisationnel*. Tome III, De Boek.

Commission of the European Communities. (2001). *Green paper promoting a European framework for corporate social responsibility*. DOC/01/9. Brussels.

Coyle-Shapiro, J., & Parzefall, M. (2008). Psychological contracts. In C. L. Cooper & J. Barling (Eds.), *The Sage handbook of organizational behavior*. London: Sage Publications.

Crozier, M. (1963). *Le phénomène bureaucratique*. Paris: Le Seuil.

Crozier, M. (1978). Attitudes of French managers regarding the administration of their firms. *International Studies of Organization and Management, VIII*(3), 39–63.

Crozier, M., & Freiberg, E. (1977). *L'acteur et le système*. Paris: Editions du Seuil.

Garriga, E., & Melé, N. (2004). Corporate social responsibility theories: Mapping the territory. *Journal of Business Ethics, 53*, 51–71.

Giddens, A. (1976). *New rules of the sociological method*. New York: Basic Books.

Giddens, A. (1984). *The constitution of society*. Cambridge: Polity Press.

Goldman, A., & Rojot, J. (2003). Negotiation. *Kluwer Law International*. New York.

Gregory, K. (1983). Native views paradigms. Multiple cultures and culture conflicts in organizations. *Administrative Science Quarterly, 28*(3), 359–376.

Hall, R. T. (1959). *The silent language*. New York: Doubleday.

Hall, R. T. (1969). *The hidden dimension. Man's Use of space in public and private*. London: Bodley-Head.

Hall, R. T. (1976). *Beyond culture*. Garden City: Anchor Press.

Hirst, R. (1965). *Perception of the external world*. New York: Macmillan.

Hofstede, G. H. (1980). *Culture's consequences. International differences in work related values*. Beverley Hills: Sage Publications.

Hofstede, G. H. (1991). *Cultures and organizations. Software of the mind*. New York: Mc Graw-Hill.

Institut de l'Entreprise. (2002). *L'entreprise et les Cadres*. Paris.

Johnson, G. (1988). Rethinking incrementalism. *Strategic Management Journal, 9*(1), 75–91.

Kluckholn, F. R., & Strodtbeck, F. L. (1961). *Variations in value orientations*. Evanston, IL: Row, Peterson.

Lederach, J. (1995). *Preparing for peace. Conflict transformation across cultures*. Syracuse, NY: Syracuse University Press.

Lynn Meek, V. (1988). Organizational culture. Origins and weaknesses. *Organization Studies, 9*(4), 453–473.

Maurice, M., Sellier, F., & Silvestre, J. J. (1982). *Politique d'Education et Organisation Industrielle en France et en Allemagne*. Paris: Presses Universitaires de France.

Mintzberg, H. (1979). *The structuring of organizations*. New York: Prentice Hall.

Morin, E. (2001). Le monde comme notion sociologique. In Daniel Mercure (dir.), *Une société-monde? Les dynamiques sociales de la mondialisation*. Presses de l'Université Laval, Quebec, De Boeck.

Rojot, J. (1988). Droits collectifs et droits individuels, les situations françaises, américaines et anglaises dans. In R. Blouin & e. al (Eds.), *La Charte des droits et les Relations Industrielles*. Laval, Québec: Les Presses de l'Université.

Rojot, J. (1994). Introduction in employee rights and industrial justice. *Bulletin of Comparative Industrial Relations*. No. 28. Kluwer.

Rojot, J. (2008). Culture and decision making. In G. P. Hodgkinson & W. H. Starbuck (Eds.), *The Oxford handbook of organizational decision making*. Oxford: Oxford University Press.

Sainsaulieu, R. (1977). *L'identité au travail*. Paris: Presses de la Fondation Nationale des Sciences Politiques.

Sainsaulieu, R. (1982). *Les relations de travail à l'usine*. Paris: Les Editions d'Organisation.

Schein, E. (1985). *Organizational culture and leadership*. San Francisco: Jossey-Bass.

Schneider, S. C. (1985, July). *Strategy formulation. The impact of national culture. The case of France* (Working Papers No. 48). New York: Pace University.

Schneider, S., & Barsoux, J. (1997). *Managing across cultures*. 2nd Ed, Prentice Hall, UK.

Simon, H. A. (1947). *Administrative behaviour* (2nd ed.). New York: The Free Press orig. 1947.

Smircich, L. (1983). Concepts of culture and organizational analysis. *Administrative Science Quarterly, 28*(3), 339–358.

Trepo, G. (1975, Mars). *Mise en place d'une D.P.O. Le rôle crucial de la direction.* Direction et Gestion, 1, and Participation: Un douloureux constat d'échec. Entreprise, No. 1020.

Trompenaars, F., & Hampden Turner, C. (1997). *Riding the waves of culture. Understanding the cultural diversity in business.* London: Nicholas Brearley.

9

Middle Eastern Women in the Workplace: Between Traditional Careers and Entrepreneurship

Madonna Salameh-Ayanian and Ursula El Hage

Introduction

Major wars and political, social and economic instability in the Middle East and North African region (MENA) have stalled foreign direct investment and led to a strong decrease in tourism as well as disruption in several economic activities at regional level. Even though a few countries, such as Qatar, the United Arab Emirates (UAE), Saudi Arabia and Bahrain, are improving their international competitiveness ranking among the top 50 countries in the world, the region is still fragile and vulnerable. Rising security concerns in countries such as Yemen, Syria and Libya have also spilled over into countries such as Lebanon and Tunisia, affecting their economies. Despite the disparity in performance, major challenges are shared by all MENA countries: these include low growth and an increase

M. Salameh-Ayanian (✉)
USEK School of Business, Holy Spirit University of Kaslik, Jounieh, Lebanon

U. El Hage
Quality Assurance Department, Université Saint Joseph, Beirut, Lebanon

N. Azoury (ed.), *Business and Society in the Middle East*,
DOI 10.1007/978-3-319-48857-8_9

in unemployment, especially a growing rate of youth unemployment. According to the United Nations Entity for Gender Equality and the Empowerment of Women (2013), a total of 51% of young women were unemployed and 23% of men in the age group 15–24. It is estimated by Hoel (2013) from the World Bank that if employment rates in the MENA region do not improve, there will be 50 million unemployed men and 145 million unemployed women by 2050.

The Status of Women

It is undeniable that women have played a fundamental role throughout history; however, they remain considerably underrepresented in managerial, social and political positions. They appear to reach a middle level without being able to manage a breakthrough, thus stagnating at a place where an invisible barrier seems to exist: the so-called "glass ceiling." Research has shown that the percentage of women in top management positions/board seats does not exceed 15% at the international level; in April 2016, women were estimated to hold a minimal 4.2% of CEO positions in America's 500 biggest companies, according to *Fortune 500* (2016) magazine. Although several endeavors have been made in order to foster the role that women have, and to encourage their participation, the situation is witnessing only very slight improvements. In the Arab region, the situation is even worse: women appear to be significantly absent from strategic managerial roles in all aspects of society.

According to the World Bank report (2016), the global average for women in the labor force is about 50%. In the MENA region, it is half that, despite the fact that more and more women are better educated than before, and only 17% work in the non-agricultural sector. Moreover, the absence of women in leadership positions is clearly reflected in the data published by Bajpai et al. (2015), which shows that women hold less than 1% of executive committee and board positions in the Gulf Cooperation Council—figures that are among the lowest in the world.

Delving into the reasons behind this low rate, various factors appear to collide in order to maintain the status quo.

Two sets of factors, grouped into two main categories, lead to this disparity: general external factors that are imposed and internal factors that are unique to the women themselves. To name a few: national culture, organizational culture, education, gender bias, stereotypes, HR (human resources) policies, marital status and maternity. Facing all this, women find themselves obliged to find alternatives to capitalize on the talents they have. In order to do this, several have decided to venture into the world of entrepreneurship that seems to provide women with more flexibility and freedom to control and organize their own work, and therefore appears to be a remedy against high unemployment and stagnant economic growth.

This chapter will tackle in its first section the elements that prohibit women from further advancing in their career within organizations. The second section will address the world of entrepreneurship.

National Culture

According to Hofstede (2010), six dimensions differentiate between the culture of different nations. They are the following:

- Power Distance Index (PDI): refers to the level of equality between individuals in the same country;
- Individualism versus Collectivism (IDV): related to the level of interdependency among individuals;
- Masculinity versus Femininity (MAS): tackles competitiveness levels among individuals and the question of gender;
- Uncertainty Avoidance Index (UAI): refers to the way in which a population considers the future and the unknown, as well as its attitude towards uncertainty;
- Long-Term Orientation versus Short-Term Normative Orientation (LTO): considers the role of the past in dictating decisions about the present and the future;
- Indulgence versus Restraint (IND): focuses on whether there is pressure to control desires and impulses, and the extent to which socialization levels are favored.

The Arab region encompasses several countries that are connected in several ways: through language, religion and proximity. However, several differences are noticeable, leading to variances when the Hofstede Model is applied to each country. But in general, and on a regional level, researchers would agree that the Mediterranean countries are characterized by:

- **High power distance**: hierarchy and tall structures predominate across public and private institutions; this factor is also reflected within relationships among individuals, whereby age and relationship with parents and other senior family members as well as religious or public figures predominate. Additionally, titles, social status and income levels affect the way in which people interact.
- **Collectivistic**: individuals in this part of the world have a high sense of belonging to their group. Strong affiliation to the family or the community based on elements such as religion or political orientation is witnessed. Bonds between individuals dictate several key decisions related to succession, recruitment and other matters.
- **Masculinity:** gender disparity is highly visible in all life's aspects; women's active role in society is restricted by obligations that are imposed on them (such as household obligations) whereas men have more freedom. Men dominate the vast majority of key governmental and board of director positions.
- **Uncertainty avoidance is high:** fear of the unknown is an aspect of this population, because of the variety of codes of beliefs and of the standards of acceptable behavior that are shared, leading to high levels of uncertainty avoidance. There is, however, a clear difference between countries: in Lebanon the ratio of this component is 50, while in Saudi Arabia the score is 80.
- **Short term oriented:** Mediterranean countries maintain a strong attachment to the past while dealing with the challenges of the present and future. Traditions are core in shaping behaviors and decisions.
- **Restraint:** norms and standards largely affect acceptable behaviors within Mediterranean society; the control of desires and refraining from certain actions become part of education, and affect the way individuals think and act while imposing specific courses of action.

In the MENA region it is worth mentioning that women cannot separate their roles of daughter, wife and mother from those of employee and manager, as the pressure to perform at home and to fulfill household obligations remains incontestably their main responsibility. However, the support of partner and family constitute a major pillar in encouraging these women to continue to seek higher challenges at work. Consequently, as they are supposed to fill first and foremost their roles at home, the possibility of maintaining a work–life balance is necessary in order to enable them to achieve at work.

Organization Culture and HR Policies

In the MENA region, women constitute 24% of the workforce compared to 76% as an average across other countries; differences in salaries between individuals with the same skillsets and the same jobs demonstrate variations in favor of men.

The local culture certainly plays a role in shaping the organizational culture. Established based on the beliefs of its founder, an organizational culture ultimately aims to create a system of shared values that reflects the organization's philosophy; it is reinforced by the actions of the management team and is perpetuated by the efforts of all the people who are part of the organization. Attracting individuals who fit within organizational culture is key; to this end, HR policies and practices are fundamental in setting the tone, starting with the very early recruitment process.

HR policies and practices are considered to be the main driver for organizational advancement. They reflect the culture of the organization as instilled by its founders. Putting in place policies and practices that support work–life balance without penalizing women would help improve the chances of women to advance in their careers. To this end, "women-friendly" and "family-friendly" policies are necessary to encourage women to seek or to continue in higher positions; these include flextime, opportunities to work from home and job sharing, as well as the provision of additional services and facilities within the institutions. Even today, work–life balance schemes fail to be institutionalized and remain rather individualistic, dependent on the personal relationship of individuals with their supervisors. This is in addition to the fact that women have to interrupt their careers owing to maternity; a situation that is considered by many a disadvantage and even a weakness when compared with the dominant male players.

An organization's culture should strive to create equal employment opportunities for its employees; this is a main element of diversity that appears to be an enrichment factor for increased productivity.

Diversity

Diversity relates to any differences between members of the organization with regard to gender, race, age, socioeconomic background as well as other characteristics, and raises ethical and social responsibilities issues. Research shows that men are three times more likely to get a job than women in the MENA region; wage variation also exists, with the balance falling more towards the men, as women appear to be underemployed. It is worth mentioning that the MENA region showcases one of the highest underemployment rates in the world for its young women, as mentioned in the Silatech report on the topic dated 2013.

In their report, Desveaux et al. (2007) show that firms with women directors perform better than those without women on their boards; gender diversity appears as a corporate performance driver. Brammer et al. (2007) specify that when the equality of representation is greater within organizations, it relates to direct and indirect benefits that may potentially arise by reflecting on the demographic characteristics of key stakeholder groups, such as customers, employees and investors.

Organizations are now aware of the importance and benefits of diversity; however, the notion of successful careers remains associated with long working hours, attendance, necessity of travel, leadership style and much more.

Leadership Style

Gender and leadership style have been subject to several studies, whereby researchers tried to identify elements that would affect the advancement of women to key positions in society. Today we can find a high ratio of women occupying middle management positions, but they fail to make it to top management: female CEOs in the Mediterranean world are rare.

With regards to leadership style, two types are considered to distinguish men and women. The transactional leadership style characterizes individuals who are systematic and work with their subordinates on the basis of reward or punishment vis-à-vis a certain behavior, while a transformational leadership style focuses on inspirational team work and try to serve group priorities that will drive the performance of the company forward while changing things around. Although both styles have their advantages and disadvantages, each is thought to work best in a certain context and setup. Researchers, however, tend to associate women with transformational leadership styles while men tend to have a transactional style.

In his article about leadership styles of men and women in the Arab world, Yaseen (2010) states that women exceed men on four transformational scales: the attributes version of idealized influence, inspirational motivation, intellectual stimulation and individualized consideration. Arab men exceed Arab women on two transactional scales: management by exception passive and management by exception active, whereas women exceed men on contingent rewards.

Attitudes towards leadership style are regarded as being based on stereotypes, which tend to allocate certain traits and behaviors for each gender and thus constitute a basis for judging and accepting the person.

Gender Bias and Stereotypes

When occupying leadership or managerial roles, women are perceived to violate gender role expectancies because these roles are more aligned with stereotypically male qualities and thus with the male gender. Attitudes are less positive toward female rather than male leaders because of the gender bias and stereotyping: two main aspects of the glass ceiling.

Women also lack a proven history in leading organizations, thus generating ambiguity about their ability to succeed. Having this perspective in mind, one can understand that boards of directors, mostly comprised of men, perpetuate the status quo by selecting managers who look like them. Additionally, women are excluded from several networking events;

they do not participate in *majlis* or *diwaniya*, culturally important social gatherings where men informally exchange information and expand their network. Additionally, the practice of purdah or seclusion in some communities means that women are confined to work in the home or in single-sex occupations, further limiting their option and opportunities for exchange and advancement, and making it impossible to work in several industries or in a broad range of companies.

Facing this situation, historically women have understood that they need to work harder than their counterparts to prove themselves; they continue to enhance their skills, obtaining graduate degrees in larger numbers than men. Nevertheless, the balance of female and male leadership remains unequal.

It is important, however, to state that in some cases women have made a choice not to access upper level management positions—having prioritized work–life balance over career advancement. As a matter of fact, they perceive top managerial positions as hostile and unattractive places, where the individual becomes a victim of the role he or she is holding.

Career Aspiration Versus Work-Life Balance

Looking at women's internal drive, we believe that a cycle of aspiration exists; it links the marital/familial status to career advancement to create the regular path that most women will follow. This cycle could be described by the following sequence. Following graduation women are enthusiastic to take on the challenge, to succeed and to work hard to advance. Once married, the drive persists until maternity happens. With the first child, and with assistance and help, equilibrium is possible. This situation is most likely to continue until the arrival of the second child, when women start to seek a different work–life balance and where home obligations begin to lead to work absenteeism and less availability for work-related events. This is when the balance begins to lean in favor of the family. As more children arrive the balance continues to change, leading—at times—to work interruption. The possibility of succeeding arises again when children reach the age of independence and self-autonomy, giving women the hope that they can make it again; but in most cases

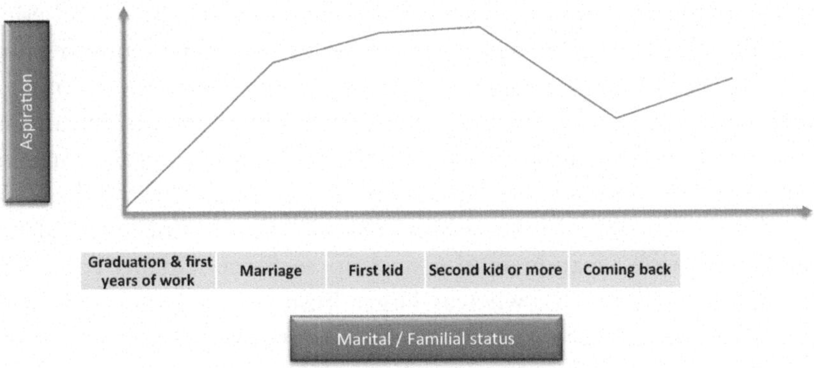

Fig. 9.1 Career path linking "Aspiration" to the "Marital & Familial Status" of women

they fail to get back on track because of the prior missed opportunities (Fig. 9.1).

Facing all these challenges, women find themselves attracted towards entrepreneurship in an attempt to overcome the obstacles and reach self-fulfillment, while at the same time coping with the requirements their gender role imposes.

Entrepreneurship as an Alternative for Unemployment

Entrepreneurship comes from the French word "entreprendre," which means to undertake. In a business context it means to start a business. The Merriam-Webster dictionary defines an entrepreneur as one who organizes, manages and assumes the risks of a business or enterprise. According to Professor Howard Stevenson from Harvard Business School (HBS), "Entrepreneurship is the pursuit of opportunity outside resources controlled." Thomas R. Eisenmann, also from HBS, explains that these opportunities face demand risk, technology risk, execution risk and financial risk.

The United Nations Human Development Report of 2015 explains that 450 million entrepreneurs have contributed to human innovation and creativity; arts and artisans have also contributed to social cohesion and cultural identity. Entrepreneurs create income for themselves, but they also recruit more people and ensure income for their entourage, which decreases general unemployment rates. Entrepreneurship can sustain economic development, which leads to growth in gross domestic product (GDP) and improved quality of life. Through viewing the effect of various national and international recessions on businesses, evidence suggests that job creation in the start-up segment remains consistent in economic downturns, whereas larger businesses are more adversely affected by external economic factors. Finally, according to Naqvi (2012), two-thirds of new jobs come from firms that are between one and five years old. According to Schumpeter, the entrepreneurial process is a major driver of economic development, and the entrepreneur is the key to economic growth.

Economic Diversification Through Female Entrepreneurship

The MENA region is home to the world's biggest energy exporters, but the drop in energy prices since 2013 has led to a need for the creation of more jobs through economic diversification and the building of a strong private sector. Female entrepreneurship is not only important for economic growth but also for economic diversification, with the study by Chalmoun et al. (2008) about the Environment for Women's Entrepreneurship in MENA demonstrating that there is a direct positive correlation between women entrepreneurs entering the economy and economic diversity. MENA countries that are looking for product diversification and alternatives for oil sales could consider promoting female entrepreneurship, so that diversification follows. The same could be said for incubators and non-governmental organizations (NGOs) that are looking for portfolio diversification.

One may observe that there is an opportunity in the MENA region for the development of healthcare and the food industry, since the region has the highest level of obese people in the world according to the United Nations Human Development Report, with an alarming 20% obesity rate.

This shows a clear opportunity for entrepreneurs. The same can be said for the education sector, which is growing considerably in the region, with an estimation of a 48% increase by 2030 (second after Sub-Saharan Africa). The innovation, technology and creativity sector is a great space in which entrepreneurs can thrive, especially female entrepreneurs in these sectors.

An example to consider is the rise of "care of others" jobs, which has been continuously growing . The sector includes home care and care for older people, people with disabilities and children. The International Labor Organization estimates there are 53 million paid adult domestic workers worldwide, of whom 83% are women. This rising sector is highly dominated by women and can create diversification. Increasingly it is attracting the attention of international corporations, who are creating systems and tools to cater for the rising number of elderly and children alone at home.

Even though the MENA region has closed 95% of its education gender gap, and has improved educational attainment, economic participation and opportunity are still less than half way, and Iran, Jordan, Pakistan, Syria and Yemen have the five worst positions in the world in this category.

Female Entrepreneurs

In most of the MENA region countries, employment is associated with tight to full-time positions that require at least eight work hours per day. This situation becomes less favorable for women who seek work–life balance especially when they have more than one child. If one considers paid and unpaid work (office and home duties), women work 1.5 times more than men. For that reason, many women have chosen unemployment (in terms of office work) in order to take care of their families, but still they still seek alternative income and fulfilling activities. For that reason many women lean towards working from home or establishing their own businesses, which gives flexibility in workload and working hours, so that domestic responsibilities can be handled alongside the generation of additional financial support for their family. Entrepreneurship is therefore the solution.

A World Bank survey developed by Chamlou (2008) about female entrepreneurs in the MENA region showed that the widely held perception that female entrepreneurs in the region are primary in the informal and formal micro sector (employing fewer than ten workers), producing basic products or less sophisticated goods and services, is wrong. Through this survey of 5169 female-owned firms that was undertaken firms in the region, it may be seen that only 8% were micro-firms, more than 30% were classified as very large firms employing more than 250 workers and about 40% of female-owned firms were individually owned. In Syria and Morocco, more than 65% of female-owned firms were managed by the owner. Of these companies, 85% operate in the manufacturing industry and 15% in services.

Female E-Entrepreneurship

When acceptance among peers and opportunities for career advancement are scarce, entrepreneurship appears to offer solid ground for self-fulfillment and business ventures. In total, 88% of the Middle East population is active on social media platforms. These platforms have generated additional opportunities, changing the traditional business model and removing numerous barriers to entering the business world. This shift has enabled several women to reap the benefits of digitalization and entrepreneurship, moving towards the new era of e-entrepreneurship. A new category of commerce is born with fewer financial and legal implications. It appears to be more efficient in terms of value chain, as several activities are outsourced and the focus is solely on the core business.

There are examples of women who have managed to monetize their hobbies into profitable businesses, gaining a large follower base on their Instagram or Facebook accounts and expanding their ventures online. Success stories mostly revolve around fashion, accessories, beauty, handiwork and much more.

During the last years female entrepreneurship initiatives have been increasing; many such from MENA have been presented in national, regional or international conferences and competitions, with some of the latest events that have taken place in Lebanon and Dubai hosting an equal male/female participation level. Some examples of female-led initiatives are Supermama from Egypt, which aims to provide budgeting and health management information for mothers, Troche from Saudi Arabia, which helps disabled women find jobs, Mumzwold, based in Dubai, which sells more than 100,000 baby related items. In addition, MIT Enterprise Forum and Co-Founder is headed by a Lebanese women.

E-entrepreneurship provides several advantages that women look for in a job: a simplification of the number and flow of activities and flexibility for work–life balance. It also develops hidden abilities such as leadership and self-confidence, as well as an ability to act quickly and decisively.

Entrepreneurship Ecosystem

It is clear that female entrepreneurs in the MENA region are more affected by the environment and the business ecosystem than their male counterpart. If we look at Ovais's Entrepreneurship in the Middle East and North Africa: Opening the Floodgates, we find specific points that female entrepreneurs should consider in order to flourish. These are:

- **Female mentoring**: mentoring is commonly neglected in the MENA region. The role of the mentor, as a guide who shares experience and insights with the entrepreneur, especially married female entrepreneurs whose circumstances and needs have different challenges than those of single or married male entrepreneurs, is crucial to channel their efforts and build on lessons that are learnt.
- **Role model presentation**: successful female entrepreneurs' stories inspire other women and create a paradigm shift. Female entrepreneurs struggling to create a successful business while taking care of their family are motivated by hearing the stories of other successful entrepreneurs in their entourage. Searching, documenting and sharing these stories via incubators or scholars is essential to nurturing the role model driver.

- **Entrepreneurship education**: this key role is played by educational institutions all around the MENA region to promote entrepreneurs and also to help them start creating their first venture while at university. Female entrepreneurs who are highly averse to risk could learn how to manage entrepreneurial risk in a controlled environment.
- **Cultural shift**: the key factor for female entrepreneurs is the support of their family and entourage, support for innovation, change, acceptance of risk, nonconformity and acceptance of continuous improvement instead of perfection. This will start in the household, where mothers need to instill this culture among their children and spread the principles of equality. This would continue in school, universities and in the community.
- **Creation of networking spaces**: finding the correct business contact for positive economic advantage is mandatory in every type of business. This is especially critical for female entrepreneurs who are trying to maximize their use of time in order to be able to manage the balance between family and work. Creating opportunities to put them in contact with key stakeholders who are necessary to foster their business inspiration would give them further confidence and increase their opportunities.
- **Governance and ease of doing business**: government is the core stakeholder for entrepreneurs, and by creating a regulatory context that makes it easier for entrepreneurs to flourish and breaking down various complex rules and regulations, individuals would be encouraged to take their first steps. It is undeniable that in the MENA region governments have major responsibilities to review the rules that limit women's participation in the business world.

Considering that women are more risk averse than man and that they have a tendency to create business out of necessity, it may be seen that they try to avoid uncertainty that might make them lose assets or possibly fail in their ventures. They try to avoid participating in sectors where there are cumbersome as well as costly and time-consuming procedures or corruption. Therefore we notice a negative correlation between female entrepreneurs and corruption. According to the World Bank's Doing Business 2008, countries with a cumbersome business environment have fewer female entrepreneurs, while the opposite is also true. Simplifying procedures would lead to creating 33% more first-time female business owners than male.

Some recommendations that would increase the participation of women in entrepreneurship in the Middle East are as follows:

- Support local organizations in creating an incubation structure to help entrepreneurs. A strong incubation network can motivate female entrepreneurs;
- Introduce e-business and e-entrepreneurship into universities and continuous education programs;
- Improve the regulatory framework, since women are risk averse and cumbersome procedures limit entrepreneurship among women;
- Encourage public–private partnerships that support entrepreneurs throughout the region;
- Introduce practical education programs into universities so young students can have a first-hand experience in entrepreneurship while at university;

Conclusion

Affirmative actions in support of women starting, formalizing and growing their enterprises are a driver for endless economic advancement. E-entrepreneurship is undoubtedly the trend; the promotion of success stories will pave the way for other women.

We can see that several factors have to coincide in order to allow women to reach the top of organizations, with the most important one being work–life balance. However, it is undeniable that without the support of the community this won't be possible. We can conclude that the glass ceiling cannot be broken unless all stakeholders join hands to create a supportive environment that recognizes the dual role women have to play. Societies cannot grow and flourish unless women are given the chance to participate in political, economic and corporate lives. Instilling a new culture that understands and nurtures their capabilities is the key to unleashing the talent that innately exists within them.

References

Bajpai, J. V., Dave, T. V., & Bajspai, M. S. (2015). Are women better leaders? What is the final verdict?-A review of prominent studies conducted on gender leadership effectiveness. Retrieved November 2016, from http://ijcem.in/wp-content/uploads/2015/05/Are_Women_Better_Leaders.pdf

Brammer, S., Millington, A., & Pavelin, S. (2007). Gender and ethnic diversity among UK corporate boards. *Corporate Governance: An International Review, 15*(2), 393–403.

Chamlou, N., Klapper, L., & Muzi, S. (2008). *The environment for women's entrepreneurship in the Middle East and North Africa*. Washington, DC: World Bank Publications.

Desvaux, G., Devillard-Hoellinger, S., & Baumgarten, P. (2007). *Women matter: Gender diversity, a corporate performance driver*. New York: McKinsey.

Fortune 500 (2016). *The percentage of female CEOs in the Fortune 500 drops to 4%*. Retreived from http://fortune.com/2016/06/06/women-ceos-fortune-500-2016/

Hoel, A. (2013). *Missing voices: Gender equality in the Arab world.* World Bank. Retrieved November 2016, from http://www.worldbank.org/en/news/feature/2013/03/14/missing-voices-gender-equality-in-the-arabworld

Hofstede, G. (2010). Geert hofstede. *National cultural dimensions*. Retrieved November 2016, from https://geert-hofstede.com/national-culture.html

Naqvi, O. (2012). Entrepreneurship in the Middle East and North Africa: Opening the floodgates. *Innovations, 7*(2), 11–17.

Women, U. N. (2012). United Nations entity for gender equality and the empowerment of women. *UN Womens Safe Cities Global Initiative*. Retrieved November 2016, from http://www2.unwomen.org/-/media/headquarters/attachments/sections/library/publications/2012/un-women-ar-2012%20pdf.pdf?v=1&d=20141013T121503

World Bank Report. (2016). Retrieved November 2016, from https://blogs.worldbank.org/arabvoices/ten-facts-about-women-arab-world

Yaseen, Z. (2010). Leadership styles of men and women in the Arab world. *Education, Business and Society: Contemporary Middle Eastern Issues, 3*(1), 63–70.

10

Ethical and Political Marketing in the Middle East

Charbel Salloum and Mario Sassine

Introduction

Political marketing, an ultimate communication weapon that is described as '*médiacratique*', became one of the bases of the control and power of states and governments. Political communication has become a catch-all, whose simple goal is to keep control of public opinion. It is in this context that the practice of ethics is questioned.

This universal concern questions the power of political marketing, which seeks to accredit or discredit other powers. This 'mediacratisation' affects government activity and business, in particular highlighting their concern for visibility, especially in the control of information to manipulate mass opinion. Everyone treats social information and international policy according to the terms and interpretations of those who hold power.

C. Salloum (✉) • M. Sassine
USEK School of Business, Jounieh, Lebanon

N. Azoury (ed.), *Business and Society in the Middle East*,
DOI 10.1007/978-3-319-48857-8_10

Ethics and political marketing are two elements that do not often go together, because all shots are allowed to reach the goal, in other words emotional manipulation and misinformation may contribute to a victory. Since the revolutions in the Arab world, the media, through making a commitment to the revolutionaries in their editorials, have questioned misinformation coming from and political ethics of Western countries. In fact, world citizens expect a transparent and ethical approach to politics based on values and beliefs and not on the manipulation of information and the media.

Political Marketing

At all times, from ancient Rome onwards, politicians have tried to be the center of attention, while counting on emotional appeal instead of facts. Political marketing emerged for the first time in 1754, during Franklin's presidential campaign for the US presidency. He used a photograph of a snake cut into pieces to represent the thirteen different colonies and to indicate their inseparable unity.

Since then, political marketing has grown considerably, especially in the twentieth century, with the appearance of the media in both form and substance starting with the Roosevelt campaign, which used the radio as a medium for the first time. This was followed by television during the Eisenhower presidential campaign in 1952. The first televised debate took place in 1960 between Kennedy and Nixon, turning the tide in favor of Kennedy.

Political marketing was born in Europe in the eighteenth century during the French revolution: posters were printed to reinforce the revolutionary texts and to influence public opinion. Napoleon I strived to cultivate his own image so that it was consistent with the country of Egypt. In contrast, it took thirty years for marketing through the radio to be adopted in France, in the form of political propaganda. It was especially during the Second World War that radio played an important role in this arena.

In general terms, political marketing has since evolved, transforming presidential primaries into a political show. It has become nowadays increasingly prized by political parties, candidates, and even governments.

The rule of modern political marketing was quickly established through the digital arsenal unleashed by the Internet and social networks. In less than a decade, this massive communication strategy weapon has become indispensable for states and governments that engage in a merciless war. This development is undoubtedly linked to the history of communication, or rather to the art of communication that was initiated by Franklin, Stalin, Roosevelt, and Goebbels—all of whom used political propaganda to manipulate public opinion. History has shown over and over again that this type of communication tends to move towards propaganda and the manipulation of freedom of thought.

This being said, it is noteworthy that political marketing emanates from two distinct academic disciplines: marketing and political science. The discipline allows players to design the attitudes, behaviors, and beliefs of politicians to play to the media arsenal's characteristics and mass communication. This concept of communication was designed to satisfy a political need to serve political organizations and states, to help them achieve their goals on the regional, national, and international levels. In other words, they seek to expropriate the control of public opinion in order to achieve their planned objectives.

Furthermore, political marketing remains a science that is in perpetual development as digital and social media advance (Zgheib 2005). In the political sphere it has been noted that this practice is simply a mixture of reason and emotion, demonstration and persuasion. Political communication, therefore, poisons not only politics, but citizens as well. It tends to impose a model where the citizen is no longer a critical element that feeds political debate, but a target that validates the ideas that others have as public opinion is guided. This strategy relies on achieving a communication policy that consists of an integrated approach for the design, standardization, and accomplishment of the communication process. This communication identifies three standard models: dialogue, propaganda, and marketing. Dialogue is the model that has acquired legitimacy because it generates rationality, freedom and the equality of opinions. By contrast, propaganda is a theological form of politics that affects freedom and exchange in order to influence, indoctrinate or undermine any possible opposition.

However, there is a certain analogy between marketing in politics and in trade. The government is treated as a commodity and citizens as consumers. The government therefore seeks to meet the needs of its citizens through the vote, or the purchase. Therefore, it is about political consumers more than it is about voters. Even though voters have become more demanding, more rational and more severe in judging the results achieved, it remains unethical and illegitimate to sell a government as a mere intangible product. In this context, political marketing may therefore be identified as a commercial medium whose practices are a set of purely instrumental techniques. This approach is none other than that of commercial marketing. Market surveys are just surveys, and the product is none other than the government and its program.

Therefore, we can understand that the product of a government is for sale. The sale is based on the government's ideas and purchases are based on votes. Voters must therefore recognize the utility in a product in order to invest their vote. The product's quality is based on the history of national and political institutions, and the voters' experiences, beliefs, and values. It is enough that the ideas and promises are carried out in order to measure the satisfaction with such an investment. There is no prize as such in politics given that the institution is not physically sold. Payment terms include subsidies such as grants, contributions, and so on, but the transaction currency is nothing more than the vote of the elector.

Communication has hence become the main pillar of political marketing, for political gain begins with sales through the media.

Ethics for Political Marketing

In the current environment, the values and beliefs of our governments are being challenged both at political and economic levels. Confidence is appearing to fade over time. Ethical issues and mutual respect are playing increasingly important roles in our daily lives, according to their utilitarian purpose (Ardichvili et al. 2010). Etymologically, the word "ethics" comes from the Greek word *ethos*, which means the manners and ways of acting. In Western philosophy, there are three origins of the term ethics. First, ethics is seen as a divine law which postulates that whatever God commands is arbitrarily good and ethical. Second, ethics is regarded as a theory of forms, in which non-physical forms represent the most accurate reality. This is supported by Plato, who states that he is an independent form outside God, who is the absolute archetype of morality and ethics. According to the third origin, everything is relative to the individual, in which case there can be no absolute morality. Each system of ethics depends on the circumstances of particular individuals or cultures. Ethics presents itself as a set of moral rules and values to be shared by an individual or an organization (Leung et al. 2009). The concept is simply a label that aims to transparently mark the principles by which good actions should be judged, within the constraints that relate to specific situations. Political marketing ethics is a branch of business ethics that relates to the role of ethics in decision-making by politicians (Morrell and Jayawardhena 2010). As business ethics, it must express both positive and normative recommendations. It focuses on ethics, responsibility, normative choices, commitments, and promises.

The marketing 1.0 (product-oriented) focuses on the product or service to generate interest in the consumer. As for marketing, 2.0 (consumer-oriented) focuses on the consumer to establish an emotional bond between him and the product or service. The emergence of environmental, societal, and cultural classes through the technological developments of Web 2.0 and smartphones has favored a return to values that embrace the human in its different emotional, intellectual, and spiritual dimensions. Political marketing and communication depends increasingly on the values and beliefs of the state, and hence its image regionally, nationally and internationally. Political marketing must address and justify the ethical mission of the institution, while taking into account the communication of its values, its beliefs, its commitments, and its ethics. Thus, the communication strategy must deepen the rational motivation of citizens, pushing the vote while increasing the expression of ethics and moral values. Indeed, political marketing does not only aim to establish an emotional framework for moral values but also hopes to shape a candidate's convictions and thoughts so that information may be diverted and corruption and guilt encouraged, if this is necessary. In fact, an individual's perceptions concerning the actual characteristics of a moral issue are theorized to influence that individual's intentions (Jones 1991).[1]

[1] Or moral intensity.

Besides, power is built on a foundation of thought, information, and propaganda to create a sort of common thought which tends to limit the freedom of the rational mind. The media is considered as the tool of control, giving power to the asymmetry of information and propaganda. Mental manipulation seeks to take over the minds of citizens, through the use of techniques of persuasion and mental suggestion that bypass an individual's critical sense, that is to say his ability to judge or to refuse to accept information. The media is a key element in the manipulation of public opinion, forming an oligopoly in global information and social control that separates out information, distinguishes the emotional subjects on which the attention of the public will be drawn and does not hesitate to censor the essential facts that would allow ethical and rational reasoning. The purpose of political marketing is no longer to inform but to distract, entertain, and divert the attention of the rational citizen away from certain truths, and then to impose opinions and half-truths. It is the instrument of manipulation that seeks to make companies act contrary to moral ethics. The listener becomes a target that may be influenced emotionally through media practices.

Citizens are overwhelmed by a flood of information that typically serves powerful interests in the political sphere. Strategies of distraction, disinformation, degradation, and emotions are used, rather than reflection. Political marketing is identified with a silent weapon that tends to marginalize ethics and deontology, states and political figures making Machiavellian maneuvers against all ethical decisions, via irrational emotional manipulation.

Similarly, political marketing can reflect the personal, narcissistic, and corrupt practices of candidates and elected governments. This has become a global phenomenon that discredits moral values and the beliefs of an entire system. How then can one promote the integration of ethical concern with the practices of marketing and political communication? The current political and economic scandals and their impact on public confidence and vitality of freedom of thought show that this task is essential. One of the ambitions of ethics is to foster a place for reflection, in order to give meaning to the moral and ethical values of social and political life.

Nevertheless, in view of persistent problems such as corruption, censorship, conflicts of interest, misinformation, and propaganda, we are led to wonder whether the concept of moral values is rational or irrational. A system of ethics makes creative sense, as it is not the same as morality, which brings with it prohibitions. Ethics is equated with autonomous social regulation, allowing the shortcomings of the state and law to be transcended; however, corrupt practices, lobbying, and disinformation may show the limits of self-regulatory approaches. Practices that are not corruption in the strict sense are nonetheless ethical breaches; and these are increasingly intolerable to citizens.

The Invasion of the Digital World Through Ethics

Transmutation technology and increasing information flows have transformed the international order. The advent of digital and the excitement of the web, social media, and various applications of Web 2.0 have enabled the introduction of new ways of communication. Web 2.0 is a concept that was developed in 2005 and is used to produce and publicize digital content on the Internet. This amazing development allows horizontal communication among users through interactivity, collective learning, and social networking. Using these techniques, each user is given the opportunity to be both reader and content contributor. Social media includes online applications, based on the ideology and techniques of Web 2.0, which allow creation, interactivity, content sharing, and social networking.

It is from this perspective that these practices offer policy alternatives to conventional communication through their high reactivity and upward dynamics, which enable political organizations and states to maintain their links with citizens. This new media landscape is evolving to favor two-way and multi-directional communication via these new applications, allowing the user to play a dual role: consumer and content creator. This is why the digital revolution has made a big splash in the political world. With communication's new tools and the retrieval of personal data, political marketing strategies can go much further than simply targeting, which may be distorted by social strata. These tools have become the weapons of hype and scam.

In fact, while political marketing used to address a certain professional category, the message today is customized according to the target.

Questions of order relating to ethics, corruption, and misinformation have resulted in the loss of confidence in political institutions and their representatives. Today, the political sphere, through its marketing policy, tends to invest in this new digital arsenal of strategic communication which in the last five years has improved the image of politics with unprecedented and stunning effectiveness. The Internet has become a way to compete against patronage abuses and the impoverishment of political discourse beyond geographical boundaries. Thanks to new media, speaking is not limited to a particular place or time zone. With these new communication technologies bringing new capacity for dialogue, everyone can express themselves in many different formats. Social networks and blogs have become a godsend for politicians who otherwise struggle to get a few minutes of television pictures or a column in a newspaper.

It has also been suggested that political parties, in their use of social media, seek to transmit non-critical information and promote the image of the government institution or party through hype and propaganda in order to promote discussion, debate, interaction, and political engagement of citizens. Facing a decline in participation and exchange, new ways are being sought in order to reconnect with voters and rekindle their role as representatives. The digital world allows them the distribution of large-scale messages and access to space for the coordination of their various activities. This interactive use is described as central to building a relationship of interactive trust and reciprocity. This is the reason why information and especially asymmetrical information is a source of power for political marketing. With the flexibility of customized websites and portals, with a constant use of email, videos, and blogs, political communication has become a vehicle of ultrafast and targeted traffic. These techniques continually influence individuals' emotions through a sense of belonging to a privileged circle.

The use of such resources in online communication strategies allows time to be invested more effectively and for information about the political ecosystem to be promulgated, while leaving room for initiative and responses. It is in this context that the digital canvas and social networks allow the control, management, and manipulation of the perception of citizens in a media space that is continually beset by rumors, disinformation, censorship, and destabilizing maneuvers (Tsalikis and Lassar 2009). Web tools are used to guard against these negative effects. The digital canvas thus empowers citizens to remind politicians that their mission is primarily ideological, and must be based on moral values and beliefs about social responsibility. The slightest error or contradiction in political communication is tracked in real time by citizens, activists, and journalists, who are all able to denounce disinformation.

But answers to ethical questions remain unclear regarding the use of personal data that is encrypted and decrypted on the digital canvas. Indeed, despite their privacy policies, Web 2.0 companies use them without limit and improperly in order to increase their investments. Political decisions made by subcontractors could also help to consolidate the fear of and cynicism towards political institutions and their representatives.

Political parties have to deal with these new means of communication, taking ownership of them and understanding the governing dynamics. Most descriptive models of ethical decision-making include what might be called a "trigger mechanism" (Mullin Marta et al. 2004). According to the same authors, this captures the extent of awareness that a situation has ethical implications.

The media can take a further step towards a deeper knowledge and understanding of new media space, which is constantly changing. Media players are seeing that their digital arsenal can be used as a political action tool for information dissemination, discussion, mobilization, and political activism. It can also serve as a control body and audit in order to discredit misinformation rationally, and to punish unethical practices.

Clairvoyance and Ethics in the Arab World

In recent years, the landscape of the Arab world has been marked by the disintegration of states in the Middle East and a power grab that could bring profit to the most radical Islamist elements. Instead of waiting for the collapse of these plans or, worse, betting on a diplomatic solution, the Middle East region has become the stake in a regional struggle that is focused on the geopolitics of emotions through political communication.

The collapse of regimes in Libya, Tunisia, Egypt, and Syria, with Lebanon behind the scenes of this ideological war, shows that a fairly significant upheaval of the geopolitical map of the Arab countries is underway.

The spontaneous and peaceful uprising that sparked the Arab revolution denotes the effect of propaganda and communication that is not only national and regional but also international, although the power of the militias and the presence of jihadists make the headlines. The Middle East has become a battleground where non-state actors operate in an environment where state power is questioned. Chaos is about to be replaced by a generalized civil war that is more or less creeping across the region.

The failure of models that have been imposed in the Arab world and the collapse of personal, authoritarian, and oligarchic power generated by family dynasties, whose corruption has left them unable to maintain a genuine political relationship. In many Middle Eastern countries, family and kinship relations are privileged both in the state and in civil society. They represent the primary means of access to resources. Political leaders are continually seeking to promote their own kin into public positions so they gain political support (Joseph 1996).

The marketing of political Islam adapts to the reality of daily life for those to whom it is addressed. The speech that is adopted is simple, and animated by a historico-religious background. In this respect, it is often negative towards Western states. In order to consolidate their power, these archaic regimes have greatly capitalized on their propagandist political communication strategies. According to Handy (1990), Middle Eastern executives believe that ethics is a very important contributor to their success.

However, political Islam is reviewed because the new policy in the post-revolutionary Arab world is to return to the notion of power that must be exercised by citizens without a spiritual guide. It is in this context that power is given to religious service, and religion dictates political ambitions and social grievances. The importance of religious doctrines is the most effective way in which to satisfy the political ambitions and appetites of domination and monarchical control.

When revolution began in the Arab countries in 2011, the media weapons used by politicians and states were the Internet and Web 2.0.

It is through the dissemination of videos of demonstrations and protests that Western citizens, aware of the cause, also became aware of the reality and came together to unite against governments and politicians that were depriving citizens from fundamental freedoms. In the other direction, digital media have also questioned the misinformation occurring in and political ethics of Western countries. World citizens now expect a transparent and ethical approach to politics in terms of values and beliefs, and do not wish to rely on misinformation in order to justify their actions and interventions, which of course have economic and social repercussions in their own nations.

In the matter of ethics and freedom of opinion, censorship reflects a major problem in these dictatorial systems. Censorship is one aspect of the power base, which uses propaganda and political communication techniques, often false or exaggerated, to justify military and economic intervention. Indeed, those in power justify their actions by saying they support democracy, human rights, religious freedom, and women's empowerment. But digital media have their own responsibilities to shoulder, because hoaxes or unfounded information forms subjective opinions that tend to heighten emotions and reflect a distorted reality during periods of crisis. Careful sorting by media propagandists allows us to avoid ideas that upset or mislead. Looking more closely, we discover under the falsehoods and omissions the scale of the irreconcilable interests of international political powers, thanks to the wealth of raw materials still to be found in the Arab world.

It is true that we live in an age of digital information, and we are continually influenced by waves of technology and deluges of communication. However, when a viewpoint is slightly different from those that are imposed upon us, it is called a political conspiracy! The technological development of propaganda and hype is omnipotent against all ethics of social responsibility and moral values of states, especially in times of trouble (like the one we are currently experiencing). This ignorance about reality is a conspiracy theory for some and a lie of omission for others. These political marketing practices were orchestrated during the Arab revolutions in Libya, Tunisia, Egypt, and Syria. Digital media coverage has questioned the blatant ethical problems in politics that only reflected the misdeeds of government forces.

Digital canvases have helped us to discredit in real time the speeches of politicians and statesmen, through the online posting of concrete evidence such as reports, images, videos, and films that analyze the situation. It is clear that the Arab Spring is already proving to be full of manipulation, propaganda, and lies; and what we are aware of is probably just the tip of the iceberg.

While it is true that we live in an era in which states are marketed politically, we must face the fact that we also live in an era of misinformation.

Conclusion

Political marketing, a traditional practice but revolutionized by the Internet, has changed the way in which the political system interacts with ethical practices and ethics in general. Politicians have become political entrepreneurs who strive to gain power without aligning themselves with all the moral values and beliefs of a particular government institution. Politicians cannot blame traditional media for the use of methods of disinformation and censorship. Digital platforms, although exciting, will be obliged to respect their commitments, to share their convictions, and affirm their responsibility and ethics as part of their future actions, for fear of being discredited by other social networks. Marketing has thus to be accommodated to some extent in the political world, because politicians need to be listening to the citizen-consumer. The techniques used to sell a product have been modified and adapted for politicians. They have become marketing products, and citizens are treated as consumers who need to be seduced and convinced with increasingly complex product attributes. Digital spaces therefore embody new areas for debate that could play a role in regulation and auditing of promises, censorship, and misinformation. The digital canvas is helping to spread national policy debates to neighboring countries and further afield. Political marketing on the web is an effective method for opening millions of doors, and is not a dangerous move towards client list communication. The use of these techniques means that the citizen is not distanced from this unprecedented political speech, and the Internet has mechanisms that are able to highlight any disinformation and censorship by cyber publishers.

Therefore it is difficult to judge the scale and accuracy of the links between politicians and the media. It is well known that the media loves and delights in political affairs, especially when they are faced with ethical stories, privacy, corruption, or misinformation. Consequently, the media influence opinions and influence policy. Political marketing also directs the media and adjusts the behavior and actions of the political sphere—they never act independently of each other! What is the place of ethics? In a Middle East in flux, media technologies play a moderating role in communication and political marketing. States are also adapting their marketing to the consequences of the information revolution. The use of information technology by governments in order to extend their influence to a wider public and to serve the interests of foreign policy challenges the practice of moral values, the ethics of information, and commitments and convictions. Despite this, ethics is seeming to find its place in the revolutions, thanks to the repeated efforts of governments to apply censorship.

References

Ardichvili, A., Jondle, D., & Kowske, B. (2010). Dimensions of ethical business cultures: Comparing data from 13 countries of Europe, Asia, and the Americas. *Human Resource Development International, 13*(3), 299–315.

Handy, C. (1990). Teach your children well. *Director, 43*(7), 25.

Jones, T. M. (1991). Ethical decision making by individuals in organizations: An issue contingent model. *Academy of Management Review, 16*(2), 366–395.

Joseph, S. (1996). Gender and citizenship in Middle Eastern states. *Middle East Report, 198*, 4–10.

Leung, A. S. M., Liu, X., & Liu, S. (2009). Moral schemas and business practices: The Ethics of Guangzhou migrant marketers. *Journal of Business Ethics, 88*(S1), 11–23.

Morrell, K., & Jayawardhena, C. (2010). Fair trade, ethical decision making and the narrative of gender difference. *Business Ethics: A European Review, 19*(4), 393–407.

Mullin Marta, J. K., Singhapakdi, A., Attia, A., & Vitell, S. J. (2004). Some important factors underlying ethical decisions of Middle-Eastern marketers. *International Marketing Review, 21*(1), 53–67.

Tsalikis, J., & Lassar, W. (2009). Measuring consumer perceptions of business ethical behavior in two muslim countries. *Journal of Business Ethics, 89*(1), 91–98.

Zgheib, P. (2005). Managerial ethics: An empirical study of business students in the American University of Beirut. *Journal of Business Ethics, 61*(1), 69–78.

Conclusion

Since the beginning of mankind, people have worked and lived in groups. As these groups grew, they formed societies, which are defined as groups of individuals involved in social interaction who share the same geographical territory and are subject to cultural norms and the same political authority. As these societies evolved, a greater capacity to feed and accommodate larger populations was needed. Following the industrial revolution and with the introduction of machines into the production process, people became so focused on increasing production that they disregarded the effect it had on the environment and its impact on future generations. Nowadays, after taking so much for granted in respect of the environment, people have started to realize that the time has come to wake up and initiate changes before it is too late. The impact of business on the environment and on people's lives is tremendous. Businesses need to become responsible citizens whose presence contributes to the wellbeing of the community, environment and all their surroundings.

N. Azoury (ed.), *Business and Society in the Middle East*,
DOI 10.1007/978-3-319-48857-8

In the context of this book, and after having explored the impact of business on society from different perspectives, from education to human resources to media and entrepreneurship, we can conclude that applying responsible business practices is highly intertwined with ethical conduct and corporate social responsibility (CSR) that is applied in enterprises. The concept and application of CSR represents a clear evolution of the relationship between society and business. Thus, CSR represents a holistic concept, and in order to achieve it companies need to directly link their social actions to the company's needs and demands. In this context a company can use and consolidate all its physical, human and financial resources towards applying CSR initiatives and developmental issues. In this way, CSR can be seen as a tool that assists with and leads to societal development. Ethical conduct is a mentality and culture that is relatively new to the Middle Eastern context, where managers understand it in a different private and personal context.

Therefore, the role of the private sector in developing an awareness of different business practices and their impact on the company's environment is vital. However, it is challenging to achieve this goal, mainly because of the lack of governmental supervision and the absence of clear regulations that control the application of such practices. Generally, in the Middle East, many countries still fall behind international standards of environmental sustainability and social responsibility. Nevertheless, with the rise of a new and educated generation in the region, new blood is being injected into traditional businesses and structural and cultural changes are taking place, encouraging progress towards a better world.

Businesses vary in the degree to which they accept and execute their social responsibilities, and this depends on their culture, economy, field of operation and many other factors. Therefore, the role of society is to guide businesses to engage in the most pressing societal issues. Businesses can build on opportunities and resources to create a greater business value and at the same time make considerable positive changes to society. As for educational institutions, they impact society through instilling values in students who will become future leaders in the business world, and thanks to these values will make ethical and responsible decisions. They will have vision, intellect and values that will be able to help mankind advance. This book takes the case of different countries throughout the region, including Algeria, Morocco, Lebanon, Egypt, Oman and Jordan. Businesses that succeed in creating value for their environment in these countries are regarded as national champions.

In conclusion, responsible business practices can lead to many benefits, such as increased profits, strong brand image and a sustained and solid reputation. Thus investing in social initiatives enables an organization to occupy a strong competitive advantage. Finally, the notion of being a socially responsible institution should change from obligation to necessity in their day-to-day operations.

Nehme Azoury
USEK School of Business
Holy Spirit University of Kaslik
Jounieh, Lebanon

Index

A

actions, 4, 5, 10, 11, 43, 55, 75, 82, 84–9, 106, 118, 130, 131, 143–5, 152, 153, 163, 169, 173, 175–7, 180
Africa, 18, 20, 22, 23, 54, 55, 60, 91, 95, 101, 106, 107, 114, 116–18, 159, 161
agriculture, 59, 69–71, 106, 119
Algeria, 68–71, 73, 75–8, 91, 91n1, 94, 109, 181
Arab, 17–44, 51–4, 57–60, 82–3, 88, 91n1, 92–5, 98, 98n5, 100, 101, 109, 119, 150, 152, 155, 161, 166, 173–6
Arab region, 17–30, 83, 150, 152

B

Benamor, 69–71, 74
bounded rationality, 141–4
businesses, 1–15, 17–24, 26, 27, 29, 30, 56, 81, 84–6, 88, 89, 91–124, 128, 133, 158–60, 179–81

C

challenges, 1, 2, 4, 10, 14, 18, 19, 22, 25, 26, 28–30, 36, 41, 42, 50, 53–6, 71, 73, 77, 84, 92, 93, 98, 99, 102, 108, 110, 120, 123, 149, 152, 153, 156, 157, 161, 168, 177
change, 1, 2, 4, 10, 13–15, 18, 19, 22, 24, 25, 29, 33, 56, 60, 61, 70, 81, 84, 89, 92, 119, 128, 129, 134, 135, 137, 142, 145, 156, 162, 176, 179–81

N. Azoury (ed.), *Business and Society in the Middle East*,
DOI 10.1007/978-3-319-48857-8

communication, 3–11, 15, 82, 85, 121, 134, 135, 139, 142, 165, 167–77
community, 4, 7–9, 11, 15, 18, 21–3, 25, 26, 28–30, 63, 68, 72, 82, 84, 86–9, 136, 139, 152, 162, 163, 179
competitive advantage, 10, 44, 76–8, 107, 132, 181
Corporate social responsibility (CSR), 2–5, 8, 11, 14, 19, 22, 26, 81–9, 124, 127–46, 180
creativity, 22, 28, 50, 77, 158, 159
culture, 18, 20, 21, 25, 30–44, 50, 59, 63, 68–71, 82–4, 86, 87, 93, 102, 106, 119, 127–46, 151–4, 162, 163, 169, 180

D

demography, 35, 36, 38, 56, 92, 101, 154
digital world, 55, 82, 171–3
diversity, 24, 50, 92, 93, 102, 119, 154, 158

E

economic growth, 18, 30, 68, 76–8, 91, 93, 98, 102, 107, 108, 123, 139, 151, 158
ecosystem, 4, 22, 23, 89, 161–3, 172
education, 6, 8, 13, 19, 22–30, 49–64, 75, 82, 83, 87–9, 96, 99–101, 110, 118, 120–2, 131, 137, 151, 152, 159, 162, 163, 1870
Egypt, 20–4, 51, 54, 58–60, 91n1, 92, 96, 107, 109, 161, 166, 174, 175, 181
entrepreneur, 19, 20, 22–6, 30, 67–78, 88, 96, 108, 113, 119, 149–63, 176, 180
environment, 1–3, 5–14, 18, 19, 25, 30, 49, 68, 72, 74, 77, 81, 82, 84, 86–9, 99, 106, 119, 122, 128–30, 132, 133, 135–7, 140, 142, 144, 145, 158, 161–3, 168, 169, 174, 179–81
ethics, 4, 82, 84, 87, 89, 130, 131, 165, 166, 168–77
evolution, 14, 93, 94, 100–5, 112, 115, 128, 168, 171, 174, 180
expectancy, 60, 61, 63

F

females, 13, 23, 25, 36, 38, 59–61, 99, 119, 155, 156, 158–63
future, 6, 18, 19, 21, 25–30, 33, 42, 49, 61, 63, 64, 82, 86, 87, 89, 131, 133, 151, 152, 176, 179, 180

G

gross domestic product (GDP), 18, 21, 57, 58, 93, 94, 96–8, 100, 102–4, 106, 107, 109, 110, 112, 123, 158
Gulf, 31–44, 55, 94, 150

H

health services, 19, 100
higher education, 51, 53, 55–9, 62, 63, 88, 99
human resources (HR), 31–44, 53, 101, 118, 121, 122, 128, 151, 153–4, 180

I

index, 4, 18, 20, 23, 92, 95, 98, 102, 103, 107, 110, 151
infrastructure, 53, 55, 61, 92, 104, 106, 121, 123
innovation, 8, 22, 23, 26, 30, 62, 64, 71, 77, 108–10, 112, 113, 124, 157, 159, 162

L

leadership, 20, 23, 25, 31–44, 116, 119, 150, 154–6, 161
Lebanon, 3, 12, 20, 50, 52, 54, 55, 57, 58, 60, 61, 83, 88, 91n1, 92, 94, 96, 97, 109, 149, 152, 161, 174, 181
Levant, 18, 88
literacy, 51, 52, 59, 60

M

market development, 114
marketing, 3, 4, 6, 82, 110, 140, 165–77
Mediterranean, 152, 155
mentality, 87, 180
methodology, 36, 40
Middle East, 20, 32, 49–64, 82, 83, 88, 91, 101, 149–63, 165–77, 180
Morocco, 20, 91, 91n1, 94, 95, 102–24, 119n26, 160, 181

N

national culture, 32, 135, 137, 142, 151–3

O

organizational performance, 86–7, 89
organizations, 2, 5, 17–30, 32–6, 41, 43, 44, 51, 54, 78, 84–6, 88, 89, 107, 118, 128, 132, 135–42, 144, 145, 151, 153–5, 158, 159, 163, 167, 169, 171, 181

P

policy, 13, 24, 25, 68, 72, 78, 88, 94, 107, 119, 121, 132, 138, 165, 167, 171, 172, 174, 176, 177
political marketing, 165–77
population, 1, 8, 20, 52, 53, 55, 56, 60, 92, 96, 98, 100–2, 111, 120, 123, 151, 152, 160, 179
private companies, 102, 108–23
private sector, 11, 21, 26, 34, 63, 102–8, 119, 123, 124, 158, 180
progress, 6, 50, 62, 67–78, 88, 99, 100, 102, 180

R

rationality, 141–5, 167
region, 1, 17, 31, 50, 69, 83, 91, 141, 149, 169
research, 20, 22, 23, 25, 27, 29, 32, 34–6, 44, 49, 53, 62, 72, 81, 88, 109, 121, 135, 136, 138, 150, 152, 154, 155
revolution, 25, 30, 92, 166, 171, 174,–177, 179
roles, 1–15, 27, 28, 30, 32–4, 43, 49, 58–61, 63, 64, 67, 68, 74, 78, 83, 86, 89, 92, 102, 108–22, 130, 136, 137, 140, 150–3, 155–7, 161–3, 166, 168, 169, 171, 172, 176, 177, 180

S

school, 7, 18–30, 50, 53, 55, 56, 58, 61, 62, 82, 87, 100, 120–2, 137, 138, 157, 162
sector, 3, 4, 11, 12, 17–19, 21, 24, 26–8, 34–8, 49, 51, 57, 61–3, 75, 82, 88, 91, 94–6, 102, 104–7, 109, 110, 112–14, 116, 118–21, 123, 124, 150, 158–60, 162, 180
societies, 1–15, 17–30, 49–64, 92, 93, 101, 136, 142, 163, 179
society, 2, 4–7, 10–14, 18–22, 24, 26–30, 32, 34, 43, 49, 50, 53, 56, 57, 59, 63, 64, 75–7, 81, 82, 86, 87, 108, 111, 127, 128, 130, 133, 136, 150, 152, 154, 174, 180
socioeconomic, 18, 27, 28, 154
strategies, 5, 6, 10, 17–19, 21, 28–9, 61–3, 73–4, 82, 86, 88, 92, 102, 106, 170–2, 174
strategy, 4–7, 9, 27, 29, 33, 57, 62, 73, 78, 85, 107, 108, 110, 119, 123, 137, 167, 169
structure, 2, 3, 33, 60, 61, 72, 76–8, 93, 110, 113–15, 119, 138, 140, 152, 163
sustainability, 4, 5, 17–22, 24–8, 30, 72, 87, 88, 128, 180
system, 11, 19, 32, 40, 50, 51, 61, 62, 64, 75, 110, 121, 131, 137, 138, 153, 169–71, 176

T

training programs, 120, 122
transparency, 7, 13, 21, 95

U

unemployment, 1, 5, 22, 50, 53, 54, 92, 94, 98, 99, 102, 108, 123, 131, 133, 150, 151, 157–9
UNESCO, 51, 52, 56, 60, 61

W

women, 9, 10, 13, 18, 22–4, 53, 58–61, 98, 99, 119, 119n26, 123, 136, 149–63, 175
work-life balance, 153, 156–7, 159, 161, 163
workplace, 10, 27, 149–63
World Bank, 50, 51, 55–9, 63, 68, 94–6, 98–101, 104, 106, 108, 109, 150, 160, 162

The manufacturer's authorised representative in the EU is Springer Nature Customer Service Centre GmbH, Europaplatz 3, 69115 Heidelberg, Germany. If you have any concerns regarding our products, please contact ProductSafety@springernature.com

Printed and bound by CPI Group (UK) Ltd, Croydon, CR0 4YY
22/09/2026
02221067-0001